ARPEGGIOS

BY JOE CHARUPAKORN

ISBN 978-1-57560-246-2

PREFACE

Arpeggios are the link between scales and chords, providing a harmonically rich melodic resource for both the improvising and composing musician. Using the notes of an arpeggio over its corresponding chord will provide a harmonic congruity that scales alone cannot guarantee.

This book presents the most thorough collection of arpeggios ever published for guitar. Triads, triads with added notes, and seventh chord arpeggios are displayed in one-, two-, and three-octave versions with numerous fingering options. Arpeggios that have extensions above the seventh are displayed in both their tertian construction (consecutive thirds) and in a scalar form, with all the chord tones condensed into an octave and displayed in two- and three-octave fingerings.

Arpeggios are a key element in a musician's foundation and technical development. Let this book serve as a guide to you, the creative guitarist, for incorporating arpeggios into your own playing.

—Joe Charupakorn

ABOUT THE AUTHOR

Joe Charupakorn is a guitarist, composer, and author. He earned a Master of Fine Arts in Composition from Purchase Conservatory of Music at the State University of New York, where he graduated Magna Cum Laude. Joe has also studied privately with many musical heavyweights—including jazz pianists Richie Beirach and Mike Longo, guitar legend Mike Stern, and contemporary classical composer Ruth Schonthal. He has performed around the world, in places such as Amsterdam, Nice, Barcelona, and Bangkok, and is currently active as a guitarist, composer, and teacher in the New York metropolitan area.

ACKNOWLEDGMENTS

I'd like to thank Arthur Rotfeld and Nick Russo, my editors, for their insight, patience, and guidance; and Mom, Dad, Sup, Jamie Elizabeth, and my friends for their unyielding support.

CONTENTS

Part I: Introduction to Arpeggios

Part II: Playing Arpeggios on the Guitar

Part III: Arpeggios in Standard Notation

PART I: INTRODUCTION TO ARPEGGIOS

Arpeggio Construction

This book is not a harmony text, yet some general knowledge of chord/arpeggio construction may be needed to make the best use of this book. Here is a brief overview:

First, chords and arpeggios are nearly synonymous: Chords are formed by selecting three or more notes from a scale and playing them simultaneously. Arpeggios are formed by selecting three or more notes from a scale and playing them separately. You can think of an arpeggio as the melodic presentation of a chord.

When creating arpeggios it is important to know the distance between each note of the arpeggio. The distance between two notes is called an *interval*. From one scale step to the next (C to D, for example), the interval is called a 2nd. Two scale steps away (C to E) is a 3rd, etc. Intervals have general and specific names. (The above examples, while generally being labeled a 2nd and 3rd, are specifically defined as a major 2nd and major 3rd, respectively.) There are five categories for labeling specific interval types. The first two come straight from the major scale, the remaining three are alterations.

Major = 2nd, 3rd, 6th, and 7th (These can also be seen as the 2nd, 3rd, 6th, and 7th notes of a major scale.)

Perfect = Unison, 4th, 5th, and octave. (These can also be seen as the 1st, 4th, 5th, and 8th note of a major scale.)

Minor = 2nd, 3rd, 6th, and 7th. (These are flatted versions of the major intervals.)

Augmented = A major or perfect interval raised a half step

Diminished = A perfect interval flatted a half step.

C	D	E	F	G	A	B	C
1	2	3	4	5	6	7	8

The best way to understand the construction of arpeggios is to examine the fundamental chord types.

Triads

The most fundamental type of chord is the triad (a three-note chord, usually constructed in 3rds). There are four basic triads: major, minor, diminished, and augmented.

A major triad is comprised of the 1st, 3rd, and 5th notes of a major scale:

Major = 1 3 5

C Major = C E G

To create the other triads, we alter notes of the major triad formula:

Minor = 1 ♭3 5

Diminished = 1 ♭3 ♭5

Augmented =1 3 ♯5

Though not spelled in thirds, there are other triads (in the sense that they are three-note chords), such as sus2 and sus4, in which the 3rd of the chord is replaced with a 2nd and 4th, respectively.

Seventh Chords and Beyond

Seventh chords consist of four notes. These chords are simply triads with the 7th note of the scale added. There are three basic 7th chord qualities; everything else is a modification of one of these.

Major 7 = 1 3 5 7

Minor 7 = 1 ♭3 5 ♭7

Dominant 7 = 1 3 5 ♭7

Extensions are achieved by adding other scale notes (such as the 9th, 11th, and 13th) to triads or 7th chords. *Alterations* are chromatic changes (such as ♭5, ♯9 or ♯11) made to either chord tones or extensions. Chords are named in the following order: letter name, quality, and uppermost extension (Dmaj9, for example). Altered notes are mentioned last (D13♭9, for example).

Non-Tertian Chords

Non-Tertian chords are chords that are not built in thirds. Other intervallic relationships such as consecutive 4ths (quartal) and consecutive 5ths (quintal) generate non-tertian harmony.

Arpeggio Formula Chart

ARPEGGIO NAME	FORMULA	DERIVED SCALE*
Triads		
major	1 3 5	Ionian, Lydian
augmented	1 3 #5	whole tone, augmented
minor	1 b3 5	Aeolian, Dorian
diminished	1 b3 b5	Locrian, diminished (whole/half)
sus4	1 4 5	Ionian, Mixolydian
sus2	1 2 5	Ionian, Mixolydian
Triads with Added Notes		
add9	1 3 5 9	Ionian, Lydian
madd9	1 b3 5 9	Aeolian, Dorian
6	1 3 5 6	Ionian, Lydian
m6	1 b3 5 6	Dorian, melodic minor
6/9	1 3 5 6 9	Ionian, Lydian
m6/9	1 b3 5 6 9	Dorian, melodic minor
dim7	1 b3 b5 bb7	diminished (whole/half)
Major 7 Arpeggios		
maj7	1 3 5 7	Ionian, Lydian
maj7b5	1 3 b5 7	Ionian b5
maj7#5	1 3 #5 7	Lydian augmented
maj7b6	1 3 5 b6 7	harmonic major
maj9	1 3 5 7 9	Ionian, Lydian
maj9b5	1 3 b5 7 9	Ionian b5
maj9#5	1 3 #5 7 9	Lydian augmented
maj9#11	1 3 5 7 9 #11	Lydian
maj9#11#5	1 3 #5 7 9 #11	Lydian augmented
maj9b6	1 3 5 b6 7 9	harmonic major

* For more on scales see the companion volume *Guitar Reference Guide–Scales*, ISBN 1575602458.

ARPEGGIO NAME	**FORMULA**	**DERIVED SCALE**
maj7♯9	1 3 5 7 ♯9	Lydian ♯2
maj7♯9♯11	1 3 5 7 ♯9 ♯11	Lydian ♯2
maj7♯9♯5	1 3 ♯5 7 ♯9	Lydian augmented ♯2
maj7♯9♯11♯5	1 3 ♯5 7 ♯9 ♯11	Lydian augmented ♯2
maj13♯11	1 3 5 7 9 ♯11 13	Lydian
maj13♯11♯5	1 3 ♯5 7 9 ♯11 13	Lydian augmented

Minor 7 Arpeggios

m7	1 ♭3 5 ♭7	Dorian, Aeolian
m(maj7)	1 ♭3 5 7	melodic minor, harmonic minor
m7♭5	1 ♭3 ♭5 ♭7	Locrian ♮2, Locrian
m(maj7)♭5	1 ♭3 ♭5 7	diminished (whole/half)
m9	1 ♭3 5 ♭7 9	Dorian, Aeolian
m(maj9)	1 ♭3 5 7 9	melodic minor, harmonic minor
m9♭5	1 ♭3 ♭5 ♭7 9	Locrian ♮2
m(maj9)♭5	1 ♭3 ♭5 7 9	diminished (whole/half)
m9♯11	1 ♭3 5 ♭7 9 ♯11	Dorian ♯4
m(maj9)♯11	1 ♭3 5 7 9 ♯11	Lydian ♭3
m11	1 ♭3 5 ♭7 9 11	Dorian, Aeolian
m(maj11)	1 ♭3 5 7 9 11	melodic minor, harmonic minor
m11♭5	1 ♭3 ♭5 ♭7 9 11	Locrian ♮2
m(maj11)♭5	1 ♭3 ♭5 7 9 11	diminished (whole/half)
m13	1 ♭3 5 ♭7 9 11 13	Dorian
m(maj13)	1 ♭3 5 7 9 11 13	melodic minor
m(maj13)♭5	1 ♭3 ♭5 7 9 11 13	diminished (whole/half)
m13♯11	1 ♭3 5 ♭7 9 ♯11 13	Dorian ♯4
m(maj13)♯11	1 ♭3 5 7 9 ♯11 13	Lydian ♭3
m7♭13	1 ♭3 5 ♭7 9 11 ♭13	Aeolian
m(maj7)♭13	1 ♭3 5 7 9 11 ♭13	harmonic minor
m7♭5♭13	1 ♭3 ♭5 ♭7 9 11 ♭13	Aeolian ♭5

ARPEGGIO NAME	FORMULA	DERIVED SCALE
	Dominant-Type Chords	
7	1 3 5 ♭7	Mixolydian
7♭5	1 3 ♭5 ♭7	whole tone
7♯5	1 3 ♯5 ♭7	whole tone
7sus4	1 4 5 ♭7	Mixolydian
9	1 3 5 ♭7 9	Mixolydian
9♭5	1 3 ♭5 ♭7 9	whole tone
9♯5	1 3 ♯5 ♭7 9	whole tone
9♯11	1 3 5 ♭7 9 ♯11	Lydian ♭7
9♯11♯5	1 3 ♯5 ♭7 9♯11	whole tone
9sus4	1 4 5 ♭7 9	Mixolydian
11	1 3 5 ♭7 9 11	Mixolydian
13	1 3 5 ♭7 9 11 13	Mixolydian
13♯11	1 3 5 ♭7 9 ♯11 13	Lydian ♭7
13sus4	1 5 ♭7 9 11 13	Mixolydian
7♭9	1 3 5 ♭7 ♭9	diminished (half/whole)
7♯9	1 3 5 ♭7 ♯9	diminished (half/whole)
7♭9♯9	1 3 5 ♭7 ♭9 ♯9	diminished (half/whole)
7♭9♭5	1 3 ♭5 ♭7 ♭9	Super Locrian
7♯9♭5	1 3 ♭5 ♭7 ♯9	Super Locrian
7♭9♯9♭5	1 3 ♭5 ♭7 ♭9 ♯9	Super Locrian
7♭9♯5	1 3 ♯5 ♭7 ♭9	Super Locrian
7♯9♯5	1 3 ♯5 ♭7 ♯9	Super Locrian
7♭9♯9♯5	1 3 ♯5 ♭7 ♭9 ♯9	Super Locrian
7sus4♭9	1 4 5 ♭7 ♭9	Phrygian, Dorian ♭2
11♭9	1 3 5 ♭7 ♭9 11	Phrygian Dominant
7♭9♯11	1 3 5 ♭7 ♭9 ♯11	diminished (half/whole)
7♯9♯11	1 3 5 ♭7 ♯9 ♯11	diminished (half/whole)
7♭9♯9♯11	1 3 5 ♭7 ♭9 ♯9 ♯11	diminished (half/whole)
7♭9♯5♯11	1 3 ♯5 ♭7 ♭9 ♯11	Super Locrian
7♯9♯5♯11	1 3 ♯5 ♭7 ♯9 ♯11	Super Locrian
7♭9♯9♯5♯11	1 3 ♯5 ♭7 ♭9 ♯9 ♯11	Super Locrian

ARPEGGIO NAME	FORMULA	DERIVED SCALE
13♭9	1 3 5 ♭7 ♭9 11 13	Mixolydian ♭2
13sus4♭9	1 5 ♭7 ♭9 11 13	Dorian ♭2
13♭9♯11	1 3 5 ♭7 ♭9 ♯11 13	diminished (half/whole)
13♯9♯11	1 3 5 ♭7 ♯9 ♯11 13	diminished (half/whole)
13♭9♯9♯11	1 3 5 ♭7 ♭9 ♯9 ♯11 13	diminished (half/whole)
7♭13	1 3 5 ♭7 9 11 ♭13	Mixolydian ♭6
7sus4♭9♭13	1 5 ♭7 ♭9 11 ♭13	Phrygian, Phrygian Dominant
7♭9♭13♭5	1 3 ♭5 ♭7 ♭9 ♭13	Super Locrian
7♯9♭13♭5	1 3 ♭5 ♭7 ♯9 ♭13	Super Locrian
7♭9♯9♭13♭5	1 3 ♭5 ♭7 ♭9 ♯9 ♭13	Super Locrian

Non-Tertian Arpeggios

P4+P4	1 4 ♭7	Mixolydian , Dorian
P4+A4	1 4 7	Ionian
A4+P4	1 ♯4 7	Lydian
P4+P4+P4	1 4 ♭7 ♭3	Dorian
P4+P4+A4	1 4 ♭7 3	Mixolydian
P4+A4+P4	1 4 7 3	Ionian
A4+P4+P4	1 ♯4 7 3	Lydian
P5+P5	1 5 9	Ionian, Dorian
P5+P5+P5	1 5 9 13	Ionian, Dorian

PART II: PLAYING ARPEGGIOS ON THE GUITAR

Reading Arpeggio Diagrams

The arpeggios in this book are presented in diagram form. These diagrams represent a portion of the guitar neck and show note locations and fingerings. The perspective of the diagrams is as if you are facing a guitar with its headstock pointing to your left (see the diagram below). The horizontal lines represent frets and the vertical lines represent strings. (Note: The 6th string is the thickest, lowest-sounding string.) The black dots indicate the note location *and* the fingering of chord tones. The arpeggio's tonic is always shown as a white dot.

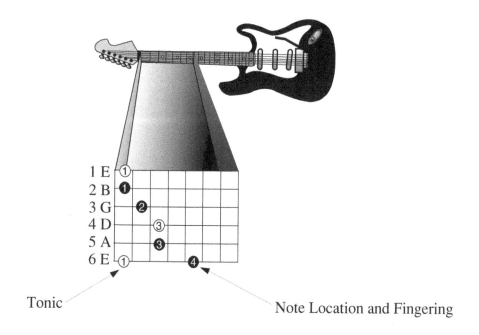

Tonic

Note Location and Fingering

Fingering Order

Of course the notes of an arpeggio can be played in any order, but when starting out, play from the lowest note to the highest note. Not only will this help you memorize the fingering, it is also the best way to hear and understand the tonal characteristics of each arpeggio.

Chord Tones

The "Chord Tones" diagram that appears on the top of each fingering page has two purposes: First, it is a master chart that shows the chord tones over the entire fingerboard. Second, it is indispensable if you are interested in playing arpeggios up-and-down the neck on a single string. Just remember that the white dots represent the root of the arpeggio and that the entire chart is moveable. (Advanced players can consult this diagram to come up with unusual or unorthodox fingerings to suit a particular musical situation.)

One-, Two-, and Three-Octave Arpeggio Fingerings

"One-Octave Arpeggio Fingerings," "Two-Octave Arpeggio Fingerings," and "Three-Octave Arpeggio Fingerings" are displayed for all arpeggios that have a 5th, 6th, or 7th as the highest chord tone.

Arpeggio Fingerings

"Arpeggio Fingerings" presents 9th, 11th, and 13th arpeggios from root to highest extension, without any repetition of chord tones.

Chord Tones in Scalar Form

"Chord Tones in Scalar Form" condenses the notes of arpeggios extended to the 9th and above into a one–octave range, with the notes arranged in a scalar, non-tertian form. Two-and three-octave fingerings are displayed.

The Arpeggios

Major

Chord Tones

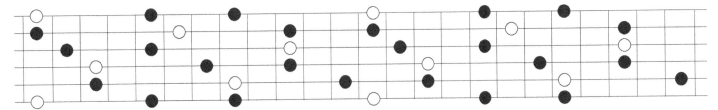

One-Octave Arpeggio Fingerings

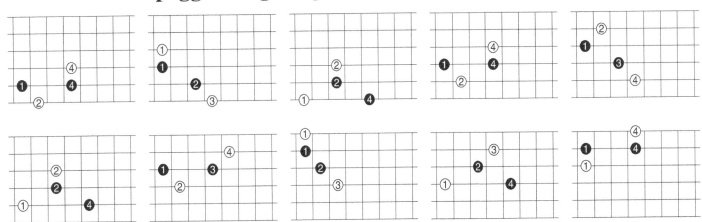

Two-Octave Arpeggio Fingerings

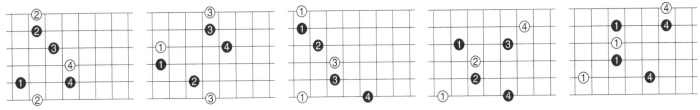

Three-Octave Arpeggio Fingerings

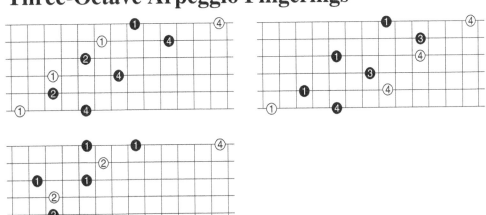

Minor

Chord Tones

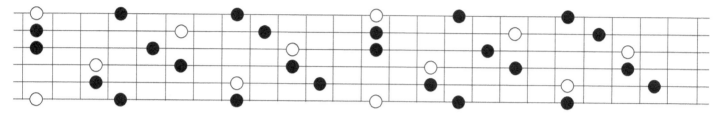

One-Octave Arpeggio Fingerings

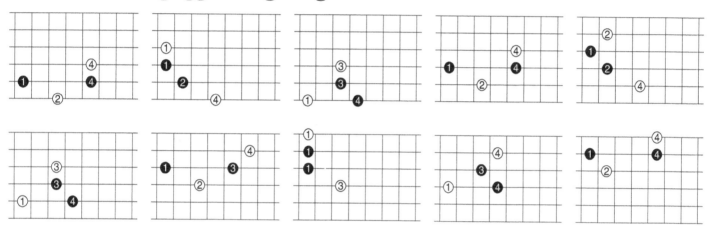

Two-Octave Arpeggio Fingerings

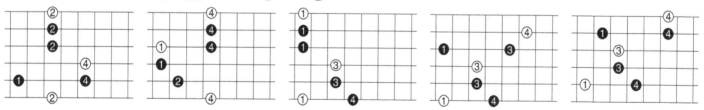

Three-Octave Arpeggio Fingerings

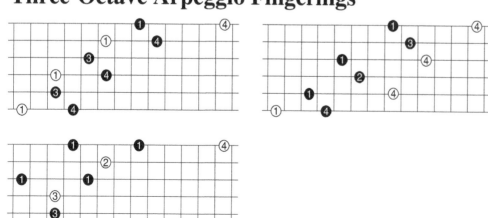

Augmented

Chord Tones

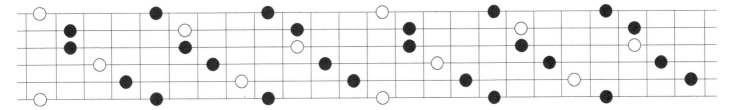

One-Octave Arpeggio Fingerings

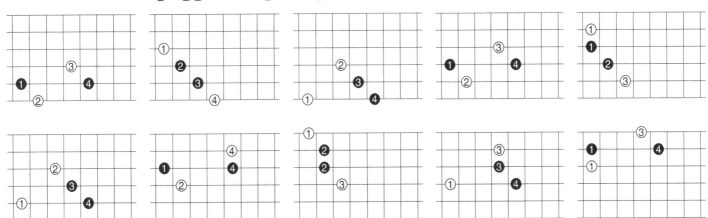

Two-Octave Arpeggio Fingerings

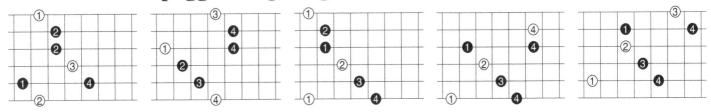

Three-Octave Arpeggio Fingerings

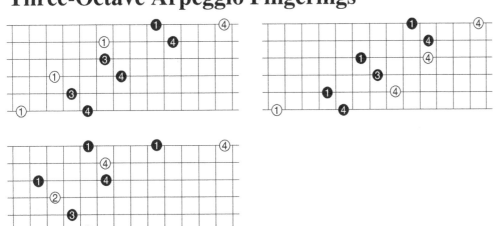

Diminished

Chord Tones

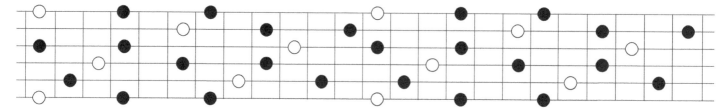

One-Octave Arpeggio Fingerings

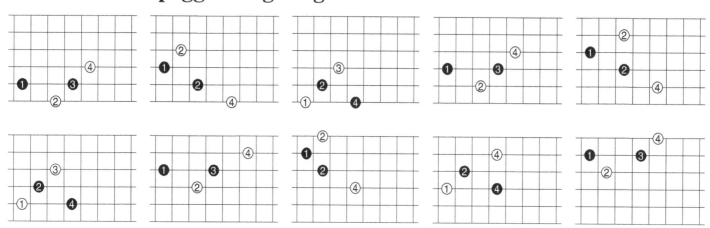

Two-Octave Arpeggio Fingerings

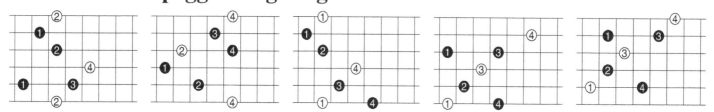

Three-Octave Arpeggio Fingerings

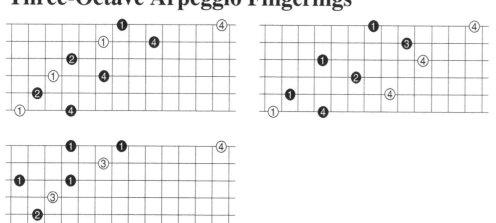

sus 4

Chord Tones

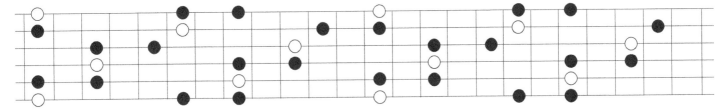

One-Octave Arpeggio Fingerings

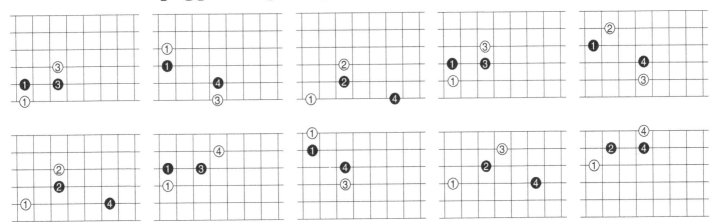

Two-Octave Arpeggio Fingerings

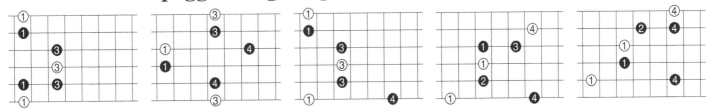

Three-Octave Arpeggio Fingerings

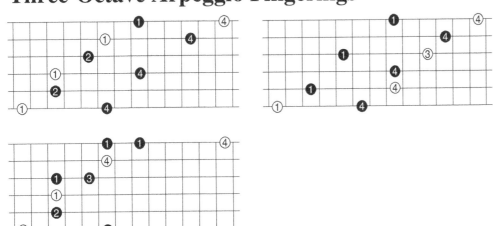

sus 2

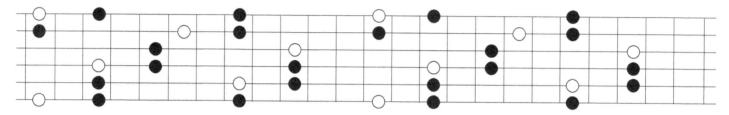

Chord Tones

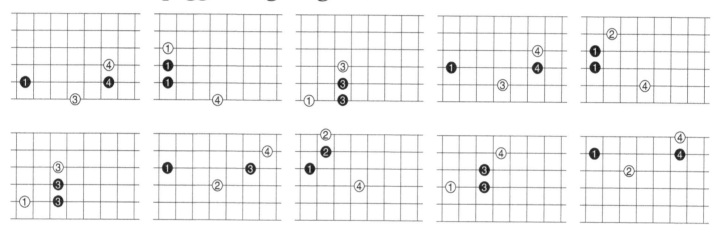

One-Octave Arpeggio Fingerings

Two-Octave Arpeggio Fingerings

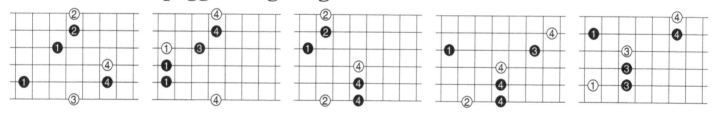

Three-Octave Arpeggio Fingerings

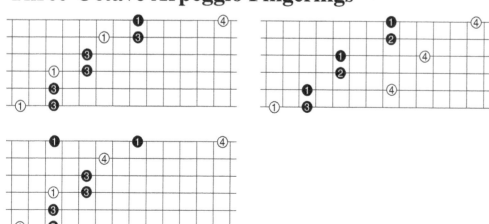

add9

Chord Tones

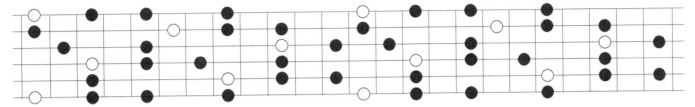

Arpeggio Fingerings

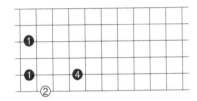 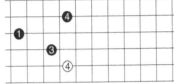 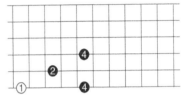

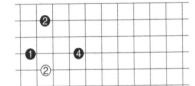 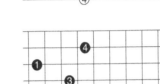 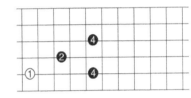

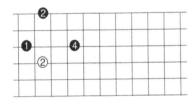 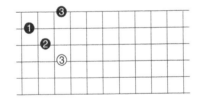 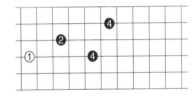

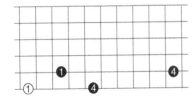 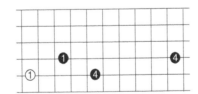 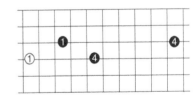

Chord Tones in Scalar Form

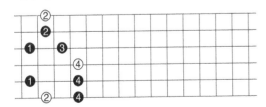 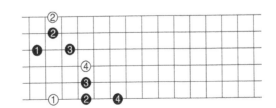

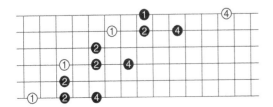 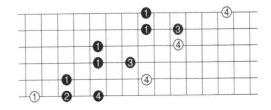

madd9

Chord Tones

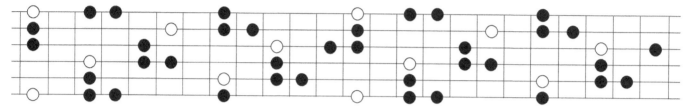

Arpeggio Fingerings

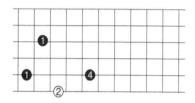
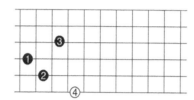
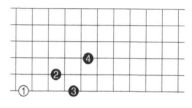

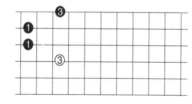
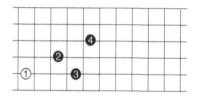

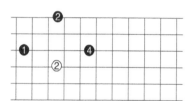
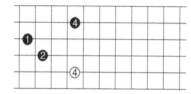
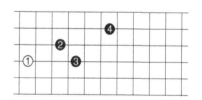

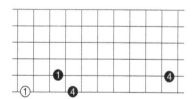
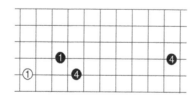
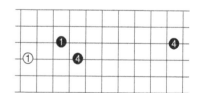

Chord Tones in Scalar Form

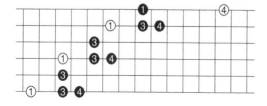
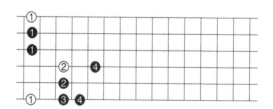

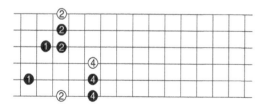
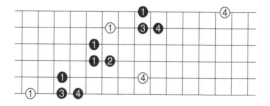

6

Chord Tones

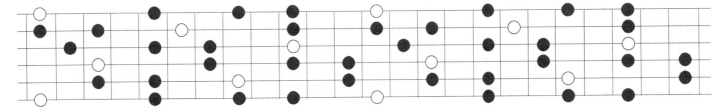

One-Octave Arpeggio Fingerings

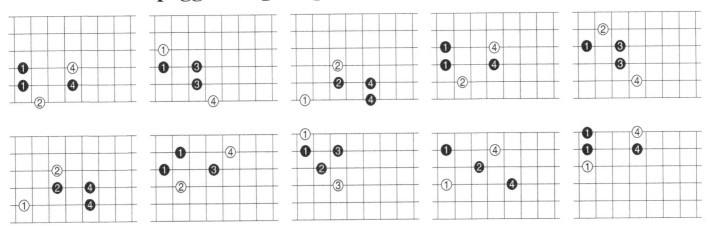

Two-Octave Arpeggio Fingerings

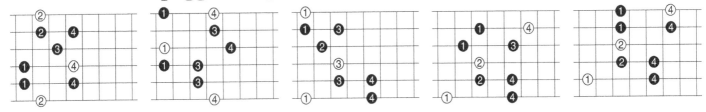

Three-Octave Arpeggio Fingerings

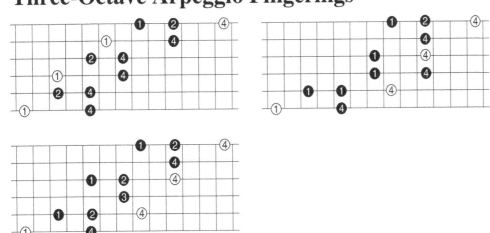

m6

Chord Tones

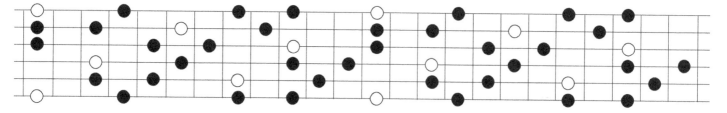

One-Octave Arpeggio Fingerings

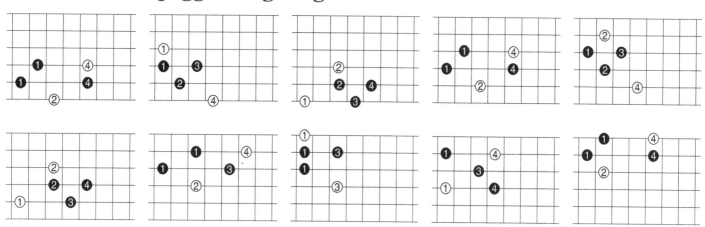

Two-Octave Arpeggio Fingerings

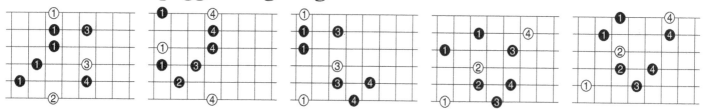

Three-Octave Arpeggio Fingerings

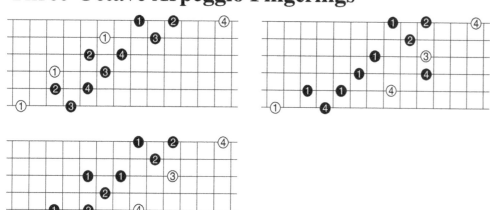

6/9

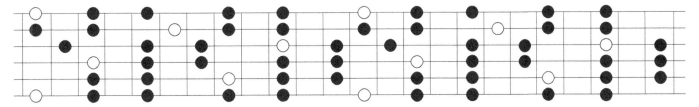

Chord Tones

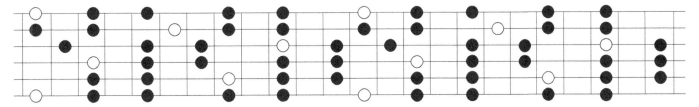

Arpeggio Fingerings

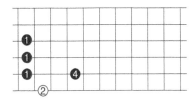
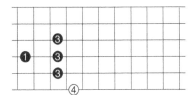
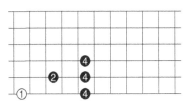

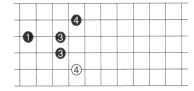
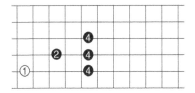

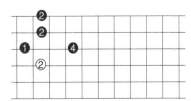
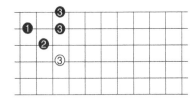
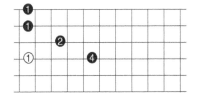

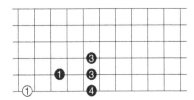
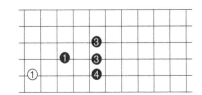
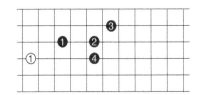

Chord Tones in Scalar Form

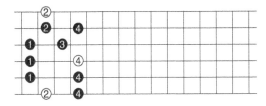
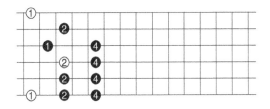

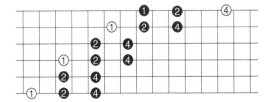
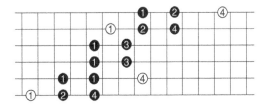

m6/9

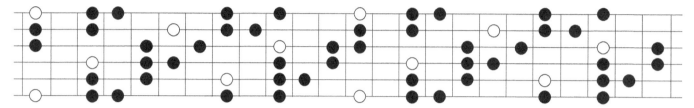

Chord Tones

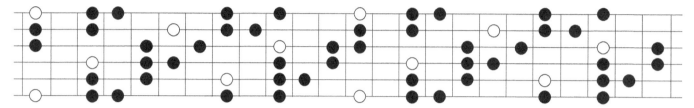

Arpeggio Fingerings

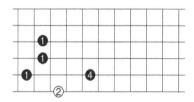
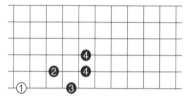

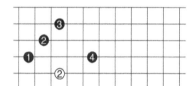
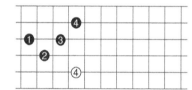
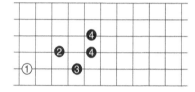

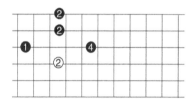
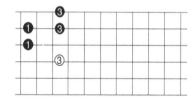
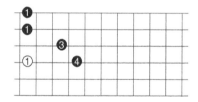

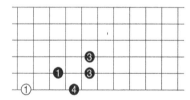
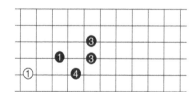
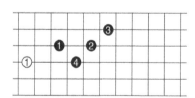

Chord Tones in Scalar Form

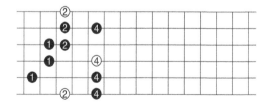
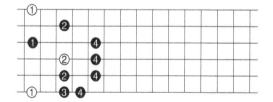

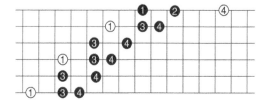
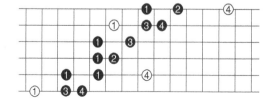

dim7

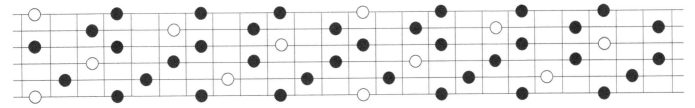

Chord Tones

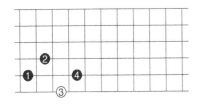

Arpeggio Fingerings

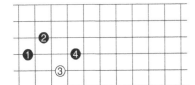
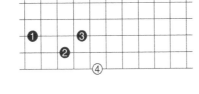
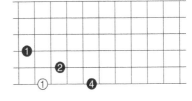

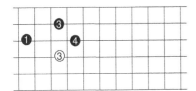
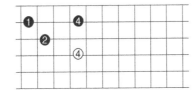
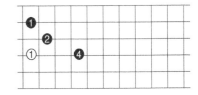

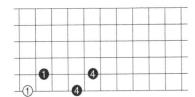
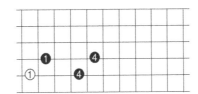
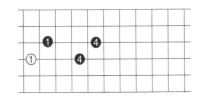

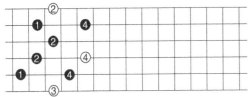
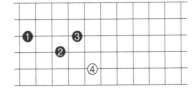
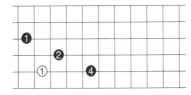

Chord Tones in Scalar Form

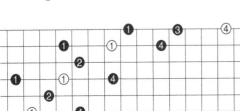
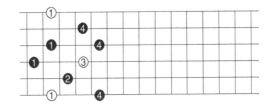

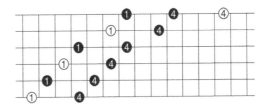

maj7

Chord Tones

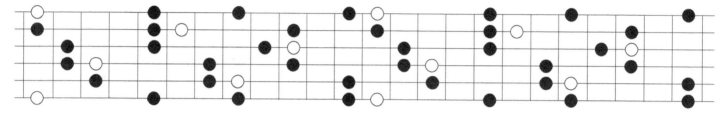

One-Octave Arpeggio Fingerings

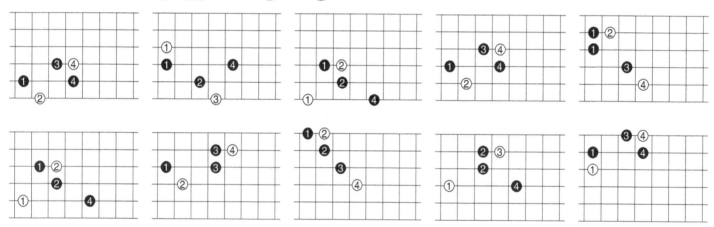

Two-Octave Arpeggio Fingerings

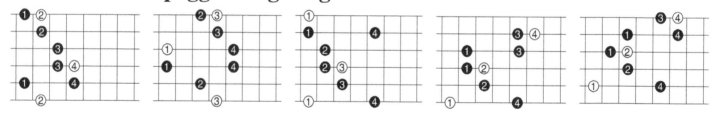

Three-Octave Arpeggio Fingerings

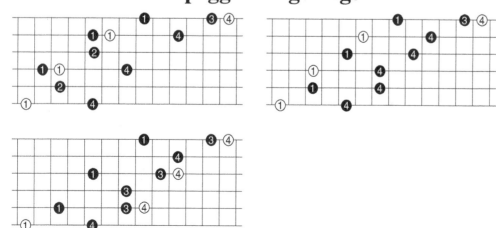

maj7♭5

Chord Tones

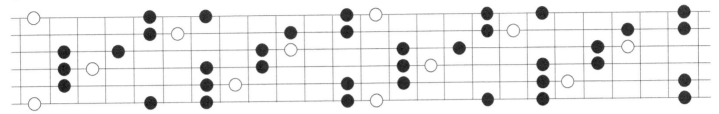

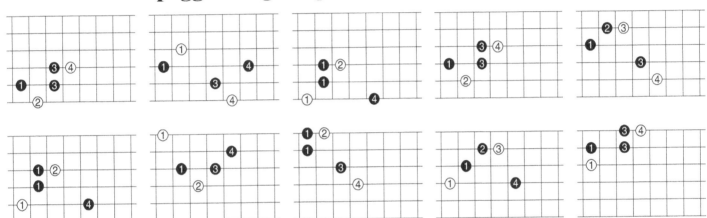

One-Octave Arpeggio Fingerings

Two-Octave Arpeggio Fingerings

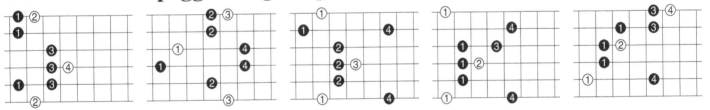

Three-Octave Arpeggio Fingerings

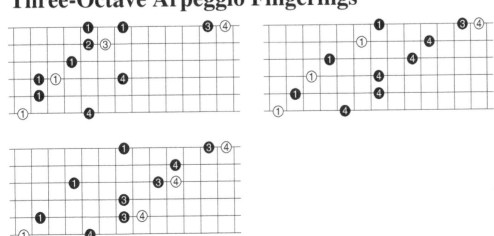

maj7♯5

Chord Tones

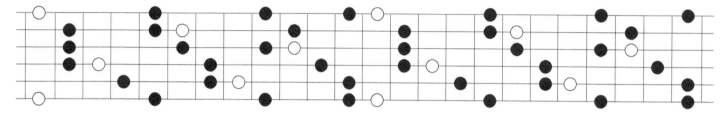

One-Octave Arpeggio Fingerings

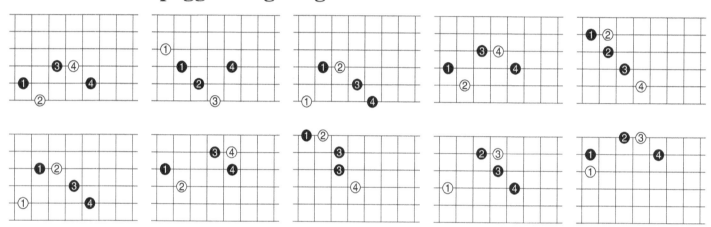

Two-Octave Arpeggio Fingerings

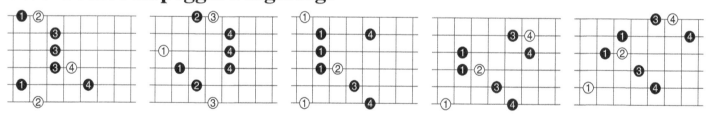

Three-Octave Arpeggio Fingerings

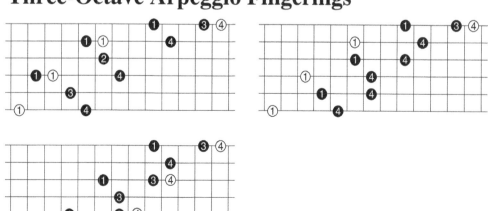

maj7♭6

Chord Tones

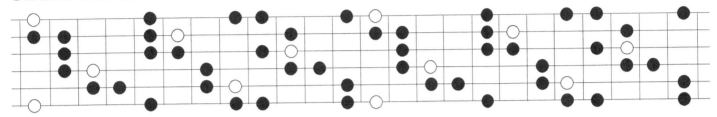

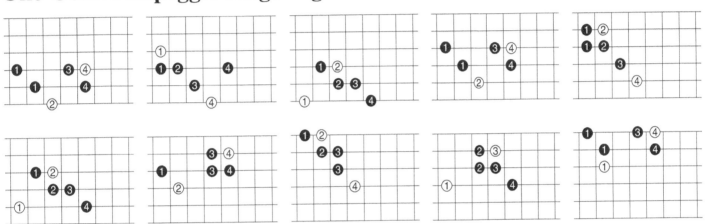

One-Octave Arpeggio Fingerings

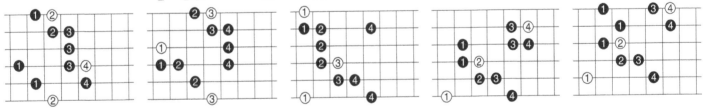

Two-Octave Arpeggio Fingerings

Three-Octave Arpeggio Fingerings

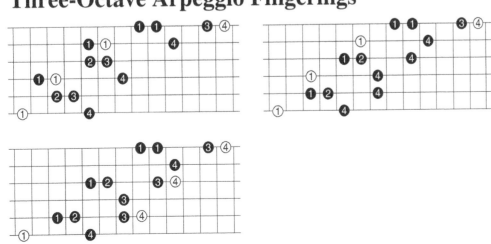

maj9

Chord Tones

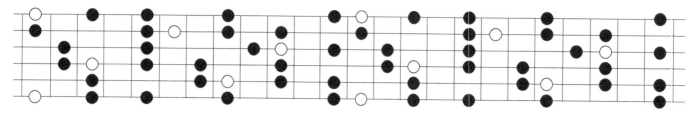

Arpeggio Fingerings

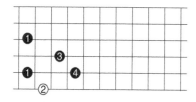
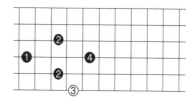
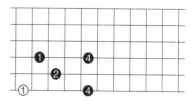

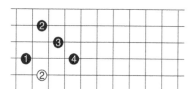
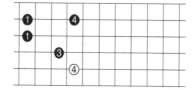
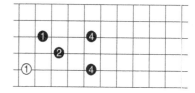

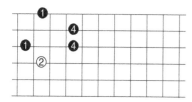
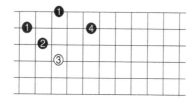
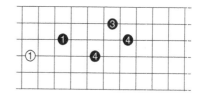

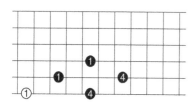
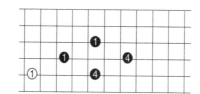
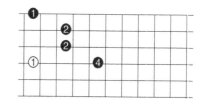

Chord Tones in Scalar Form

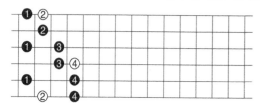
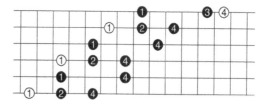

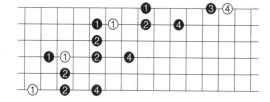
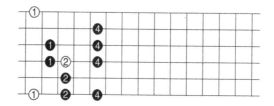

maj9♭5

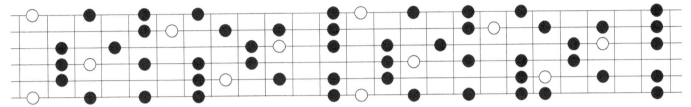

Chord Tones

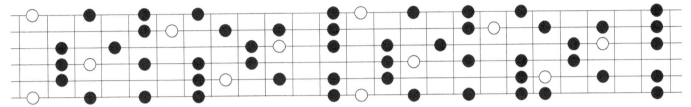

Arpeggio Fingerings

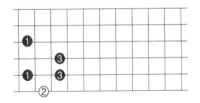
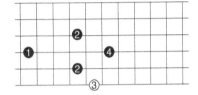
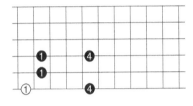

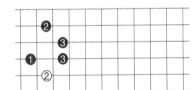
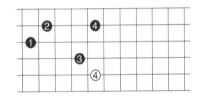
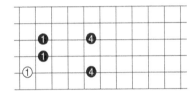

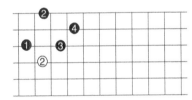
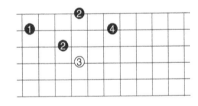
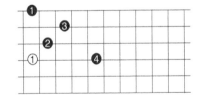

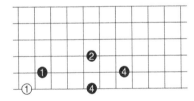
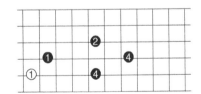
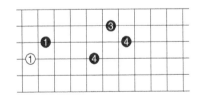

Chord Tones in Scalar Form

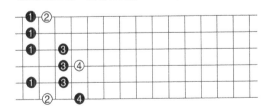
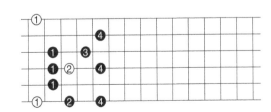

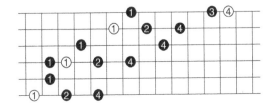
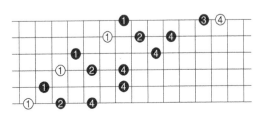

maj9♯5

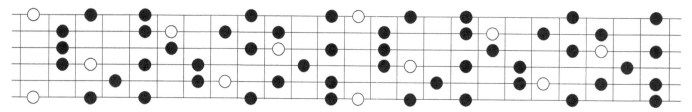

Chord Tones

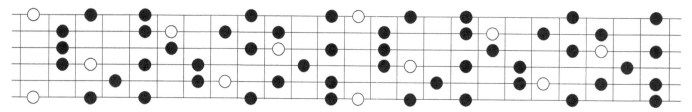

Arpeggio Fingerings

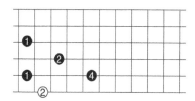
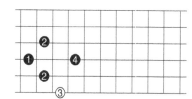
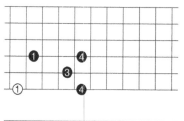

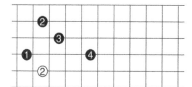
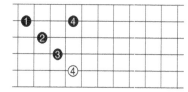
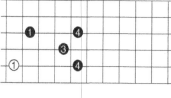

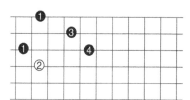
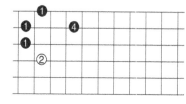
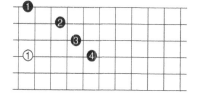

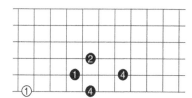
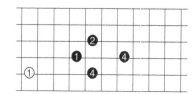
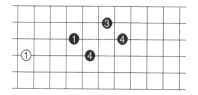

Chord Tones in Scalar Form

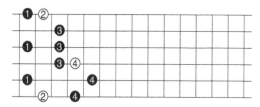
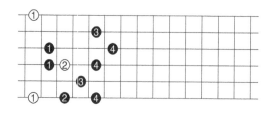

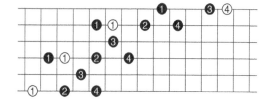
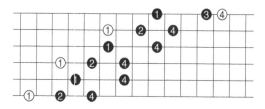

maj9♯11

Chord Tones

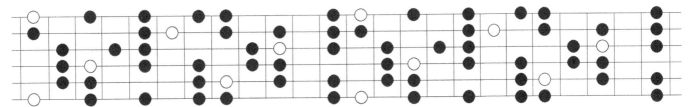

Arpeggio Fingerings

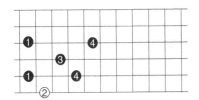  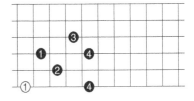

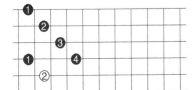 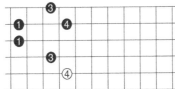 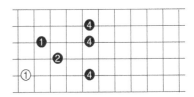

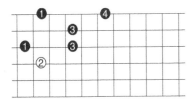 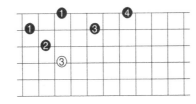 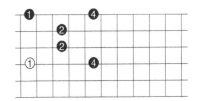

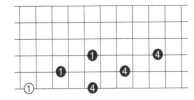 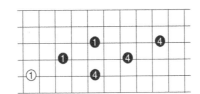 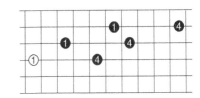

Chord Tones in Scalar Form

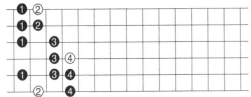  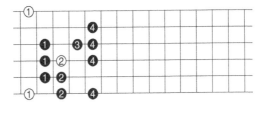

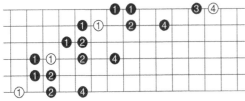 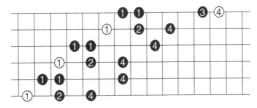

maj9♯11♯5

Chord Tones

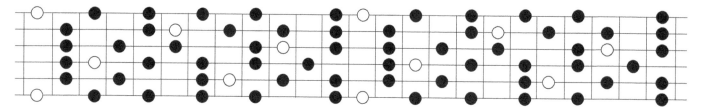

Arpeggio Fingerings

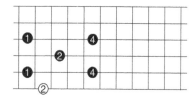
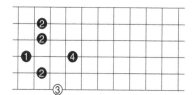
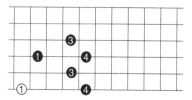

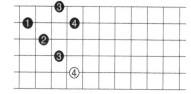
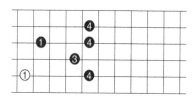

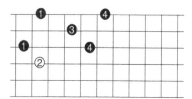
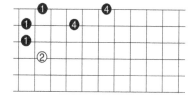
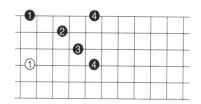

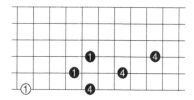
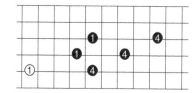
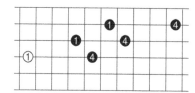

Chord Tones in Scalar Form

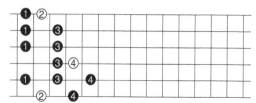
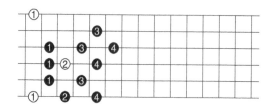

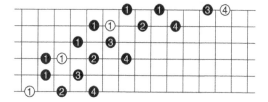
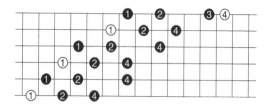

maj9♭6

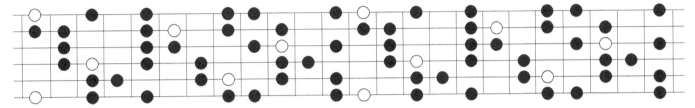

Chord Tones

Arpeggio Fingerings

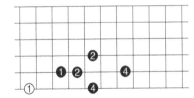
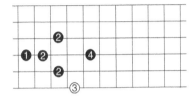
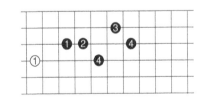

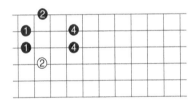
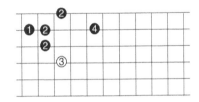
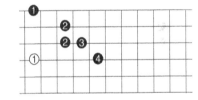

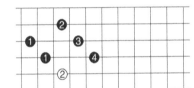
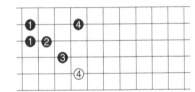
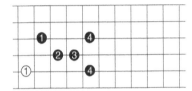

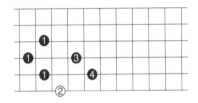
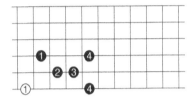

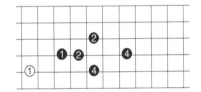

Chord Tones in Scalar Form

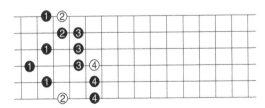
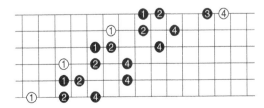

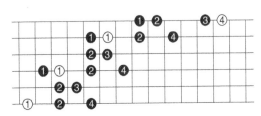
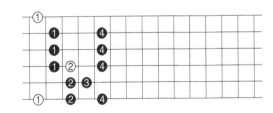

maj7♯9

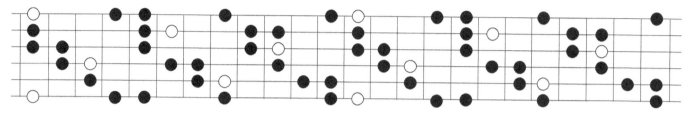

Chord Tones

Arpeggio Fingerings

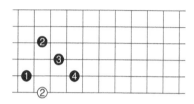 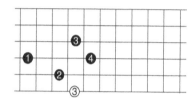 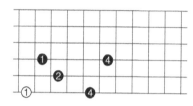

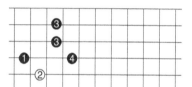 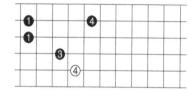 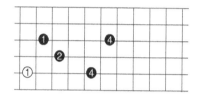

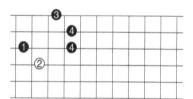 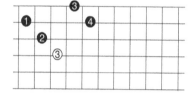 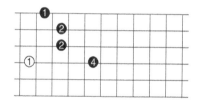

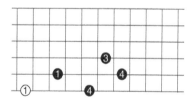 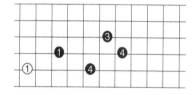 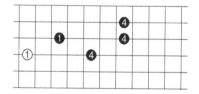

Chord Tones in Scalar Form

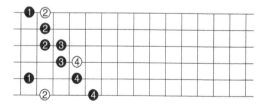 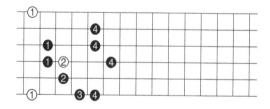

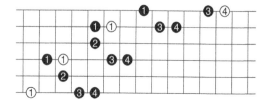 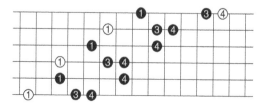

maj7♯9♯11

Chord Tones

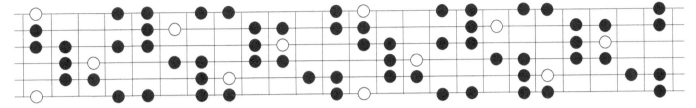

Arpeggio Fingerings

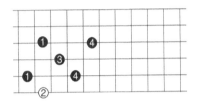 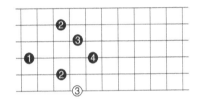 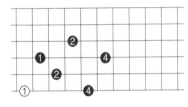

 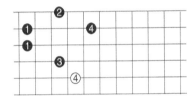 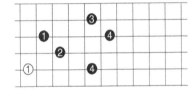

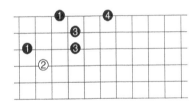 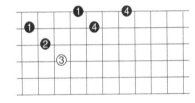 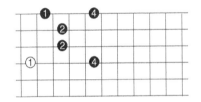

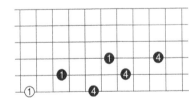 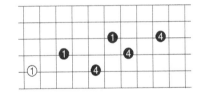 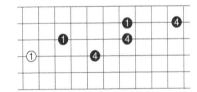

Chord Tones in Scalar Form

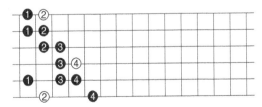 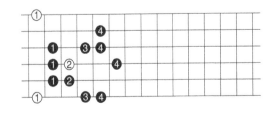

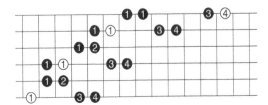 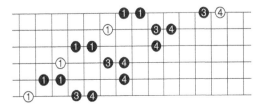

maj7♯9♯5

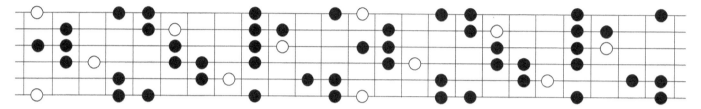

Chord Tones

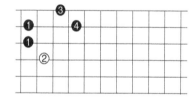

Arpeggio Fingerings

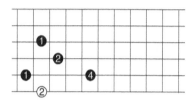
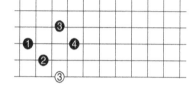
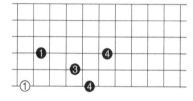

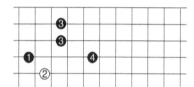
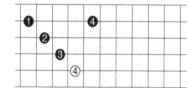
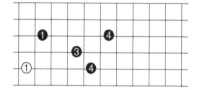

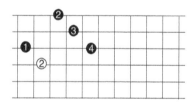
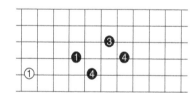
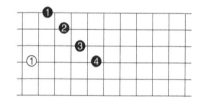

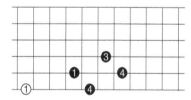
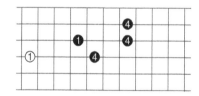

Chord Tones in Scalar Form

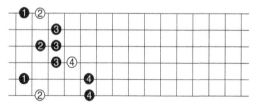
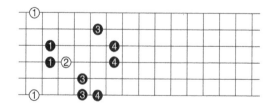

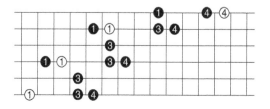
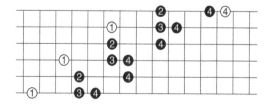

maj7♯9♯11♯5

Chord Tones

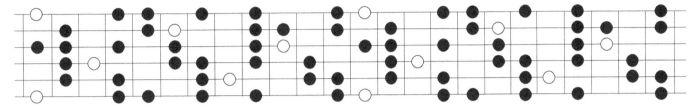

Arpeggio Fingerings

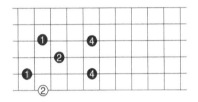
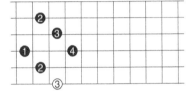
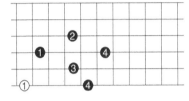

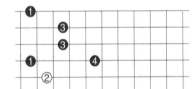
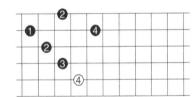
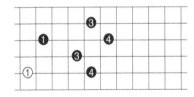

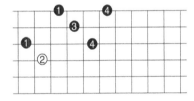
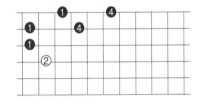
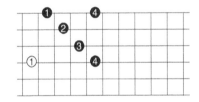

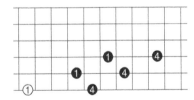
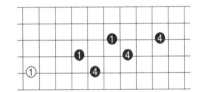
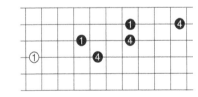

Chord Tones in Scalar Form

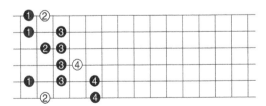
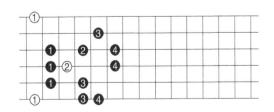

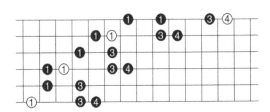
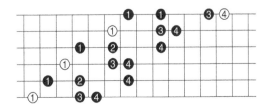

maj13♯11

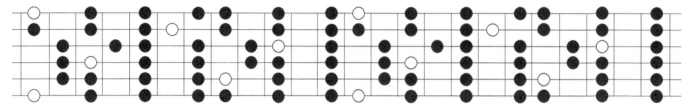

Chord Tones

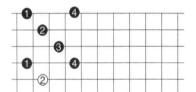

Arpeggio Fingerings

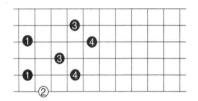
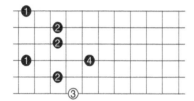
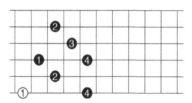

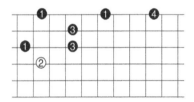
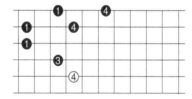
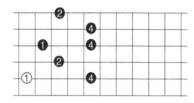

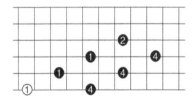
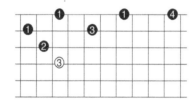
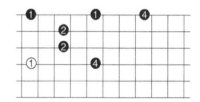

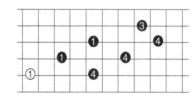
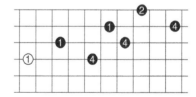

Chord Tones in Scalar Form

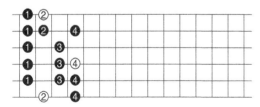
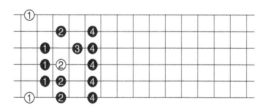

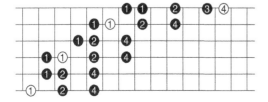
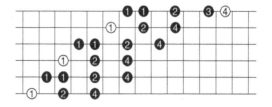

maj13♯11♯5

Chord Tones

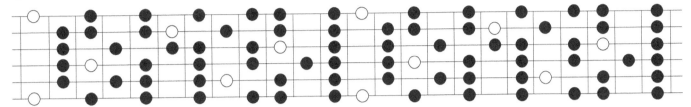

Arpeggio Fingerings

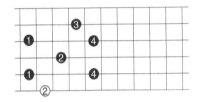 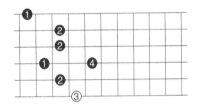 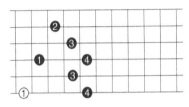

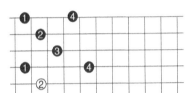 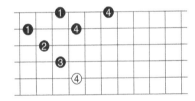 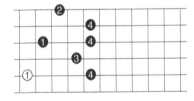

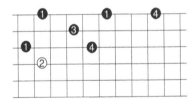 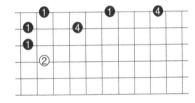 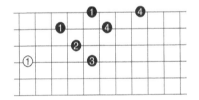

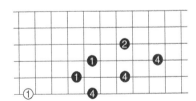 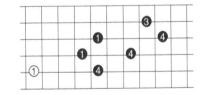 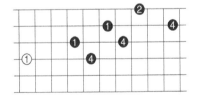

Chord Tones in Scalar Form

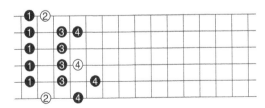 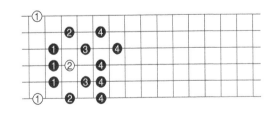

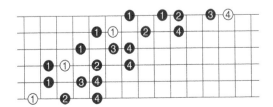 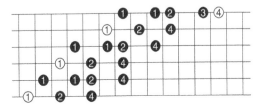

m7

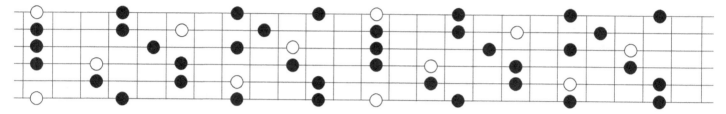

Chord Tones

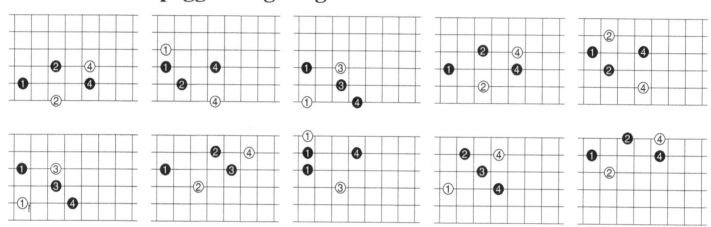

One-Octave Arpeggio Fingerings

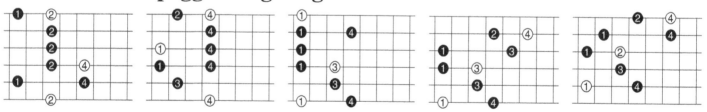

Two-Octave Arpeggio Fingerings

Three-Octave Arpeggio Fingerings

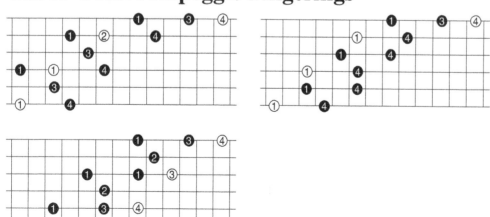

m(maj7)

Chord Tones

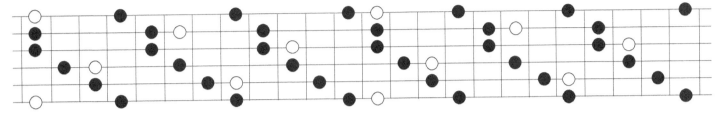

One-Octave Arpeggio Fingerings

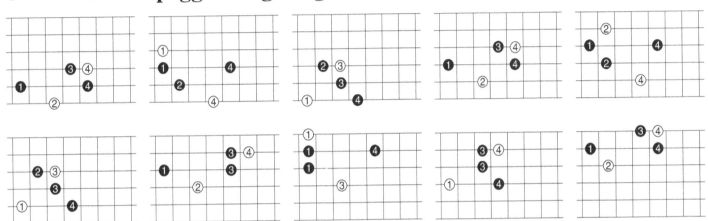

Two-Octave Arpeggio Fingerings

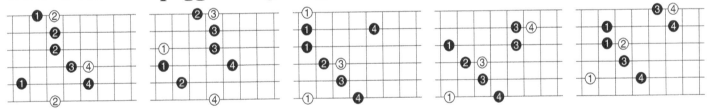

Three-Octave Arpeggio Fingerings

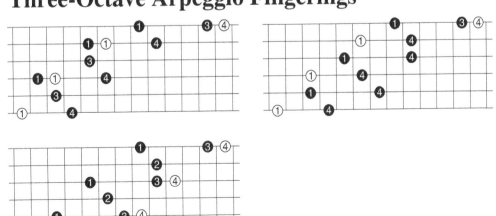

m7♭5

Chord Tones

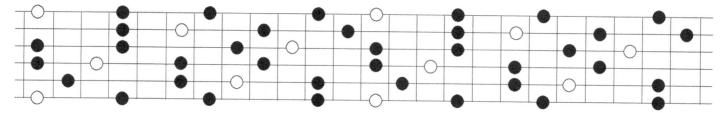

One-Octave Arpeggio Fingerings

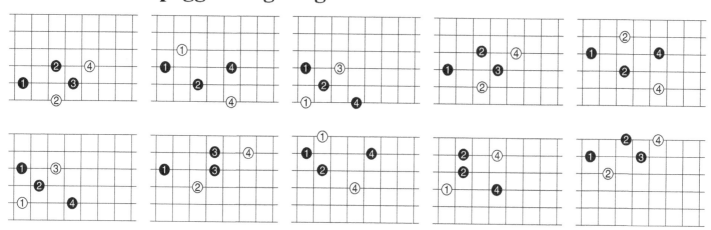

Two-Octave Arpeggio Fingerings

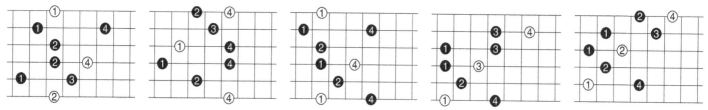

Three-Octave Arpeggio Fingerings

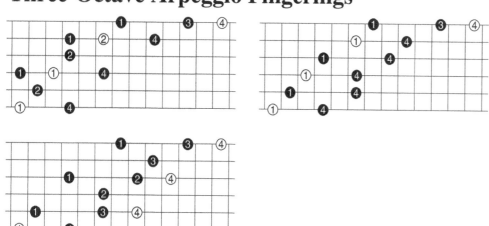

m(maj7)♭5

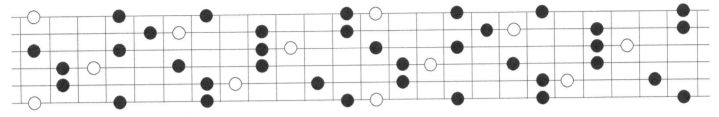

Chord Tones

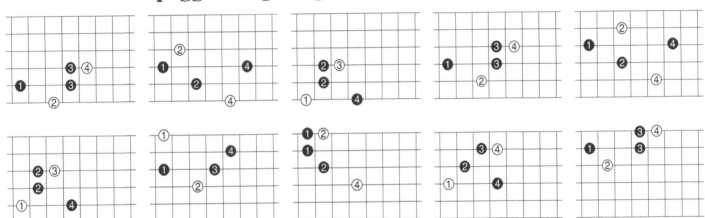

One-Octave Arpeggio Fingerings

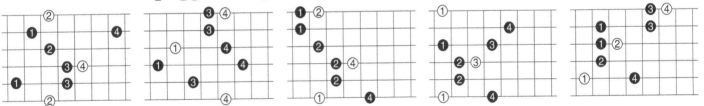

Two-Octave Arpeggio Fingerings

Three-Octave Arpeggio Fingerings

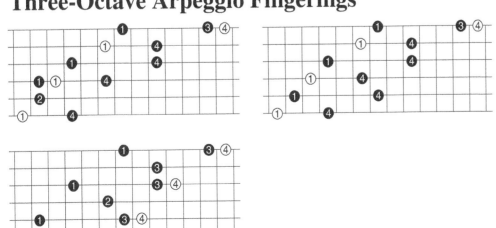

m9

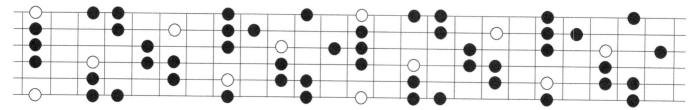

Chord Tones

Arpeggio Fingerings

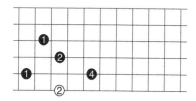
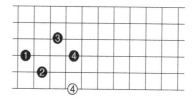
(blank)

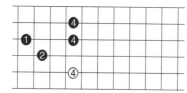
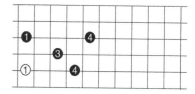

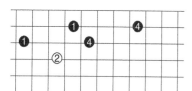
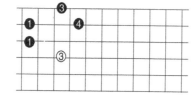
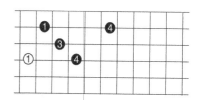

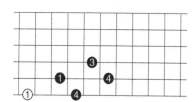
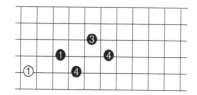
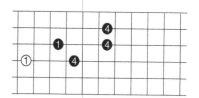

Chord Tones in Scalar Form

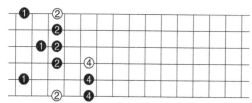
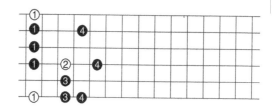

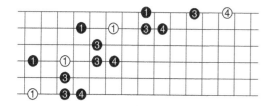
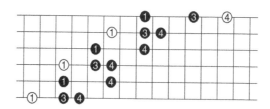

m(maj9)

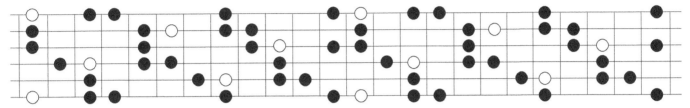

Chord Tones

Arpeggio Fingerings

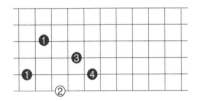 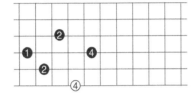 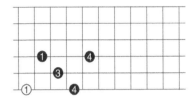

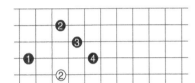 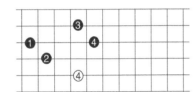 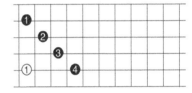

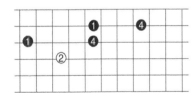 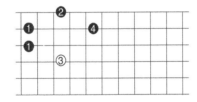 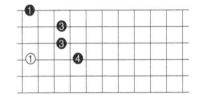

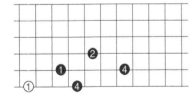 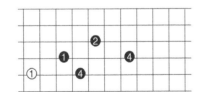 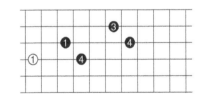

Chord Tones in Scalar Form

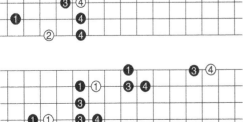 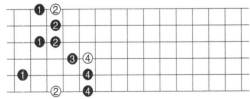

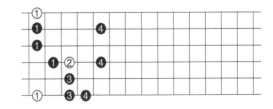 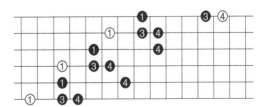

m9♭5

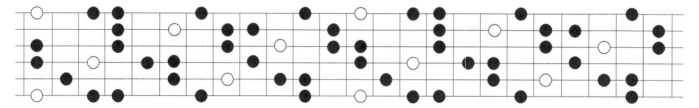

Chord Tones

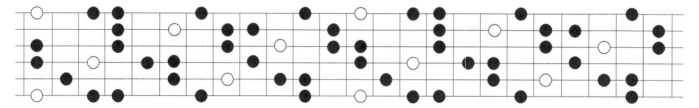

Arpeggio Fingerings

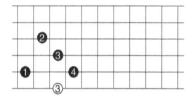
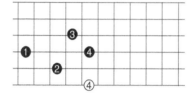
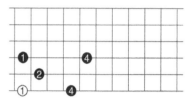

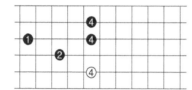
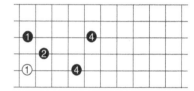

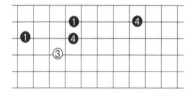
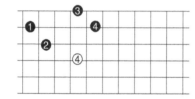
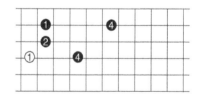

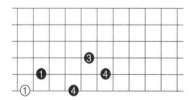

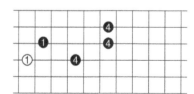

Chord Tones in Scalar Form

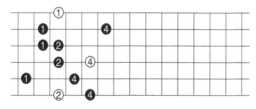
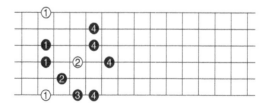

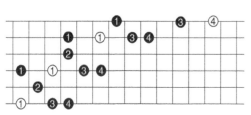
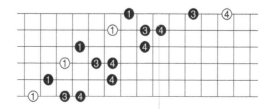

m(maj9)♭5

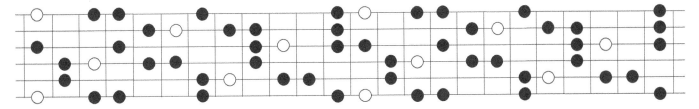

Chord Tones

Arpeggio Fingerings

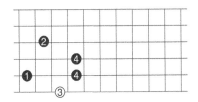
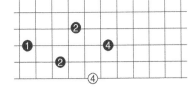
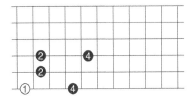

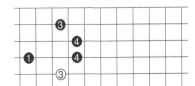
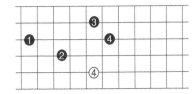
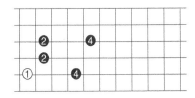

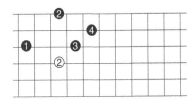
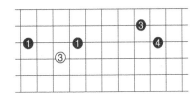
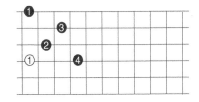

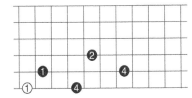
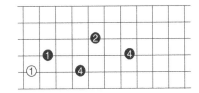
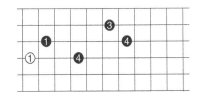

Chord Tones in Scalar Form

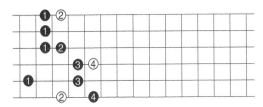
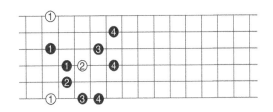

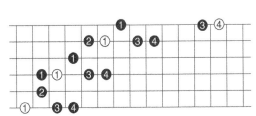
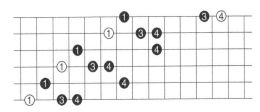

m9♯11

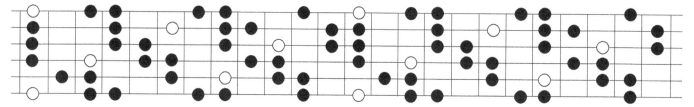

Chord Tones

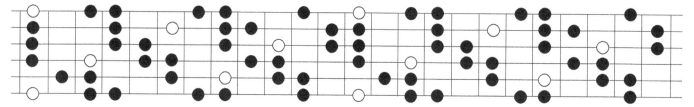

Arpeggio Fingerings

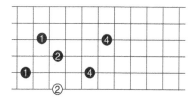
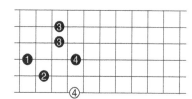
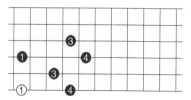

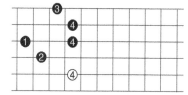
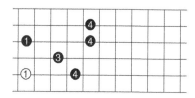

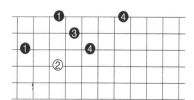
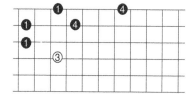
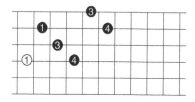

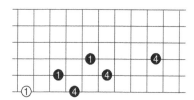
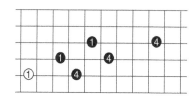
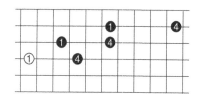

Chord Tones in Scalar Form

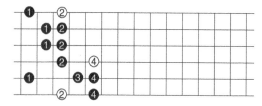
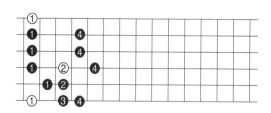

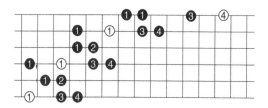
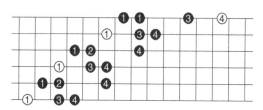

m(maj9)♯11

Chord Tones

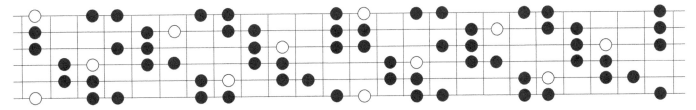

Arpeggio Fingerings

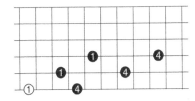 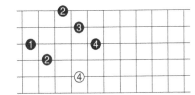 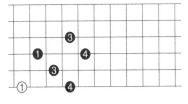

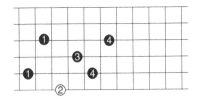 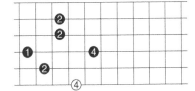 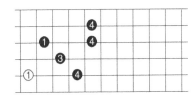

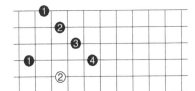 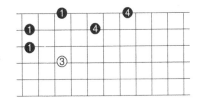 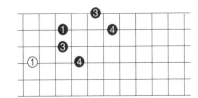

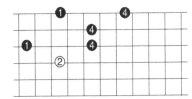 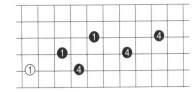 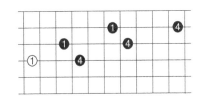

Chord Tones in Scalar Form

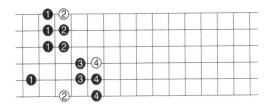 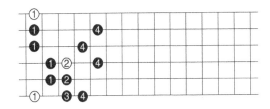

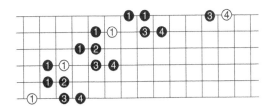 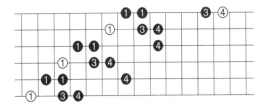

m11

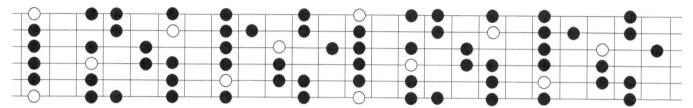

Chord Tones

Arpeggio Fingerings

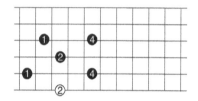 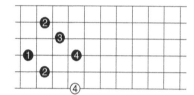 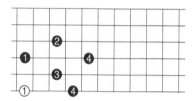

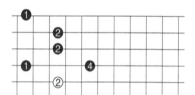 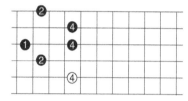 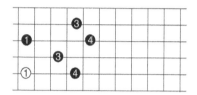

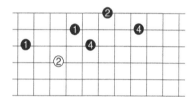 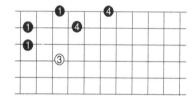 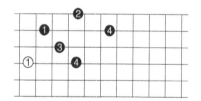

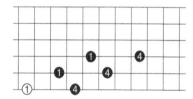 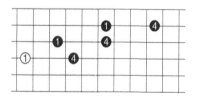 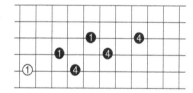

Chord Tones in Scalar Form

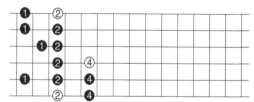 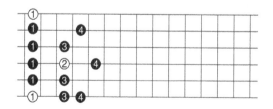

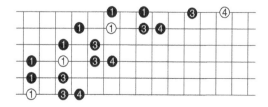 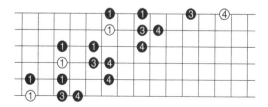

m(maj11)

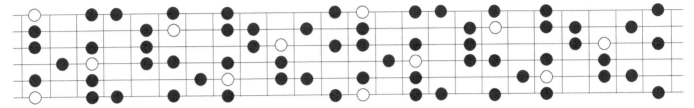

Chord Tones

Arpeggio Fingerings

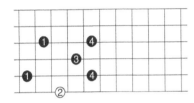 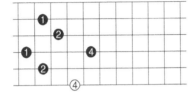 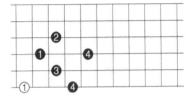

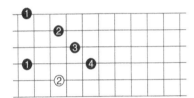 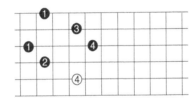 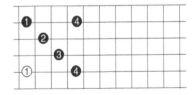

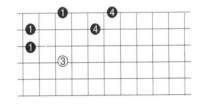 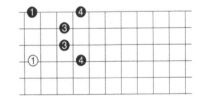

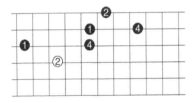 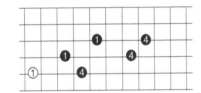 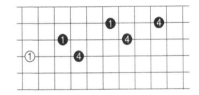

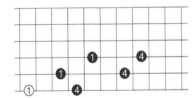

Chord Tones in Scalar Form

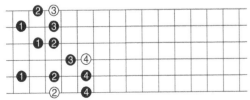 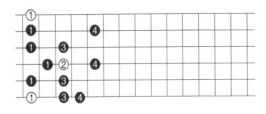

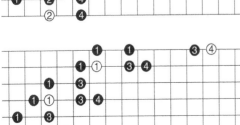 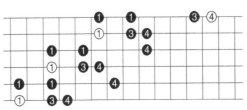

m11♭5

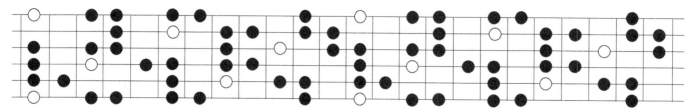

Chord Tones

Arpeggio Fingerings

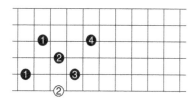
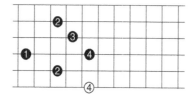
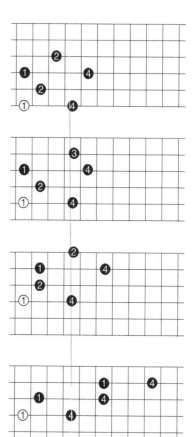

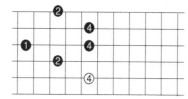

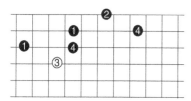
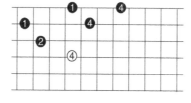

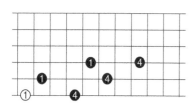
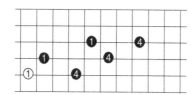

Chord Tones in Scalar Form

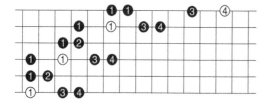
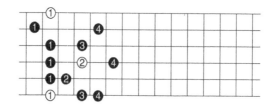

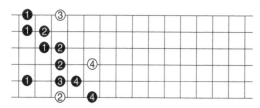
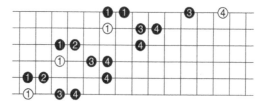

m(maj11)♭5

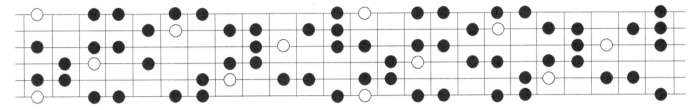

Chord Tones

Arpeggio Fingerings

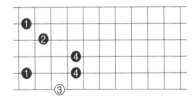 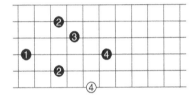 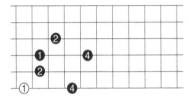

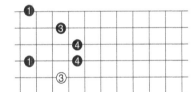 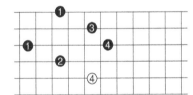 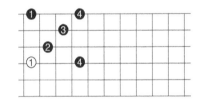

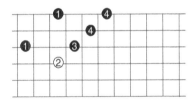 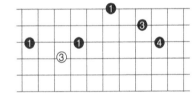 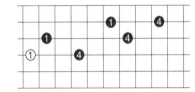

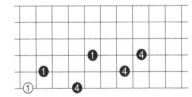 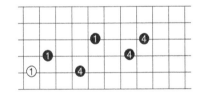 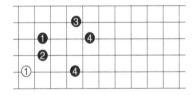

Chord Tones in Scalar Form

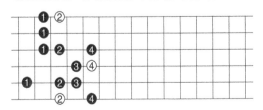 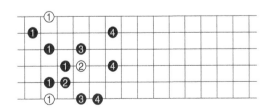

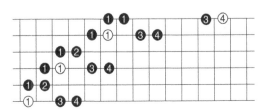 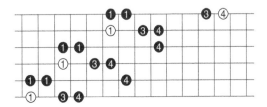

m13

Chord Tones

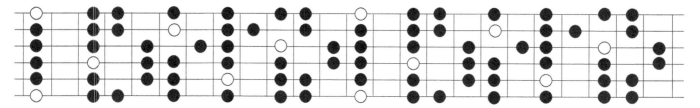

Arpeggio Fingerings

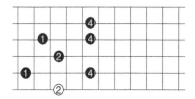
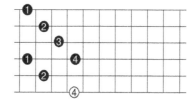
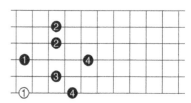

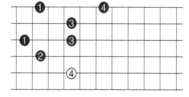
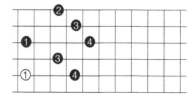

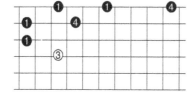
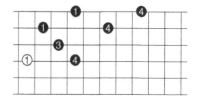

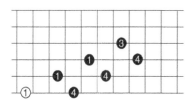
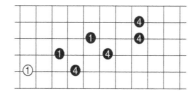
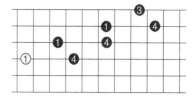

Chord Tones in Scalar Form

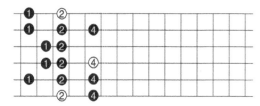
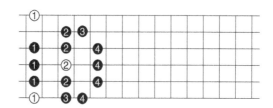

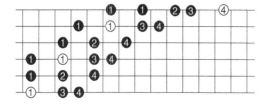
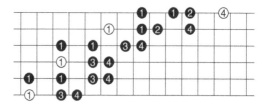

m(maj13)

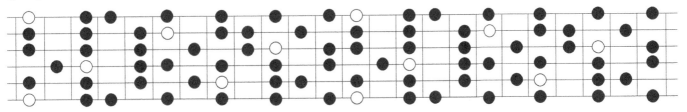

Chord Tones

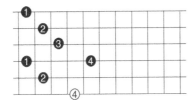

Arpeggio Fingerings

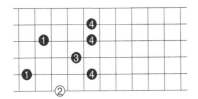

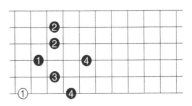

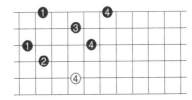
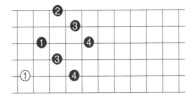

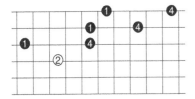
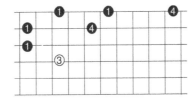
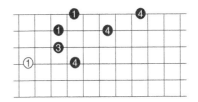

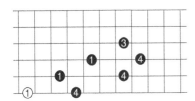
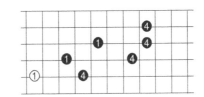
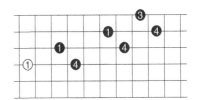

Chord Tones in Scalar Form

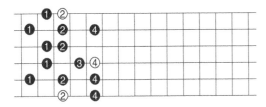
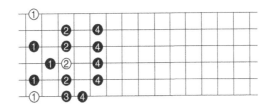

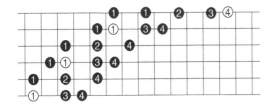
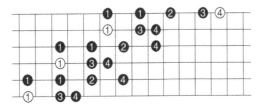

m(maj13)♭5

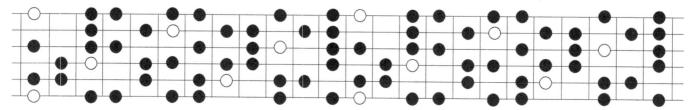

Chord Tones

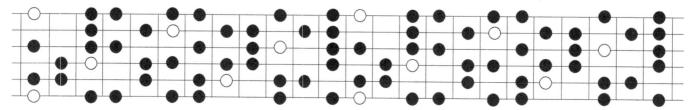

Arpeggio Fingerings

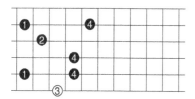
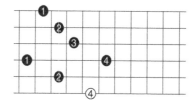
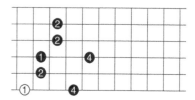

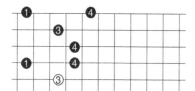
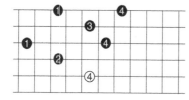
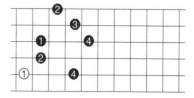

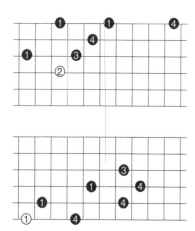
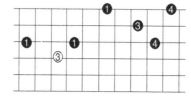
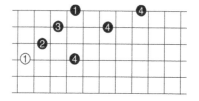

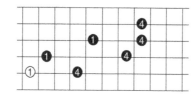
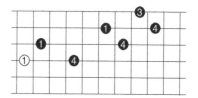

Chord Tones in Scalar Form

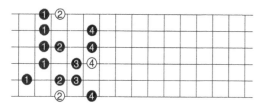
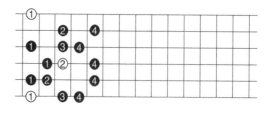

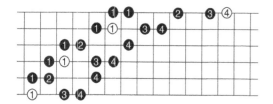
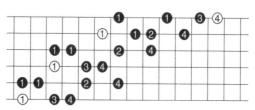

m13#11

Chord Tones

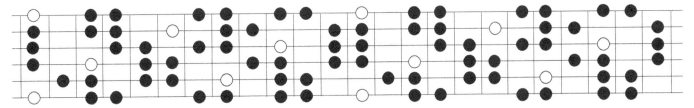

Arpeggio Fingerings

 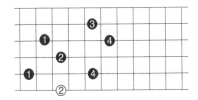 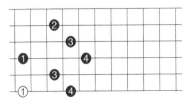

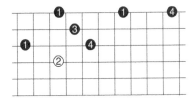 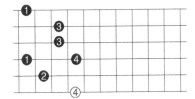 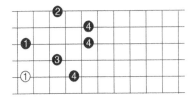

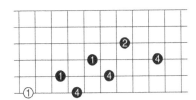 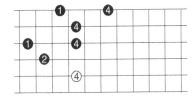 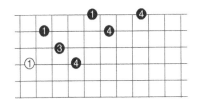

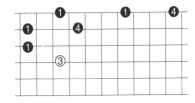 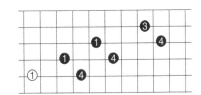 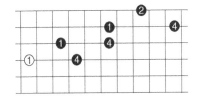

Chord Tones in Scalar Form

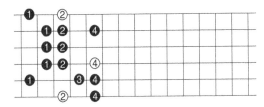 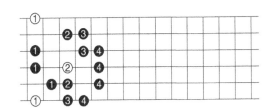

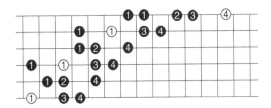 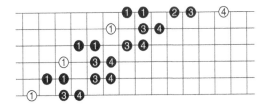

m(maj13)#11

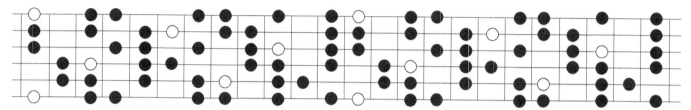

Chord Tones

Arpeggio Fingerings

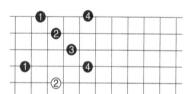
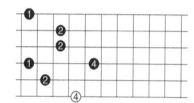
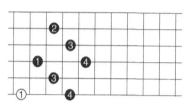

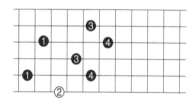
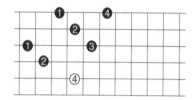
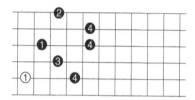

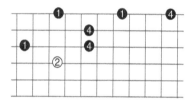
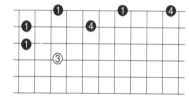
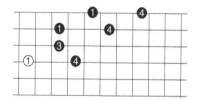

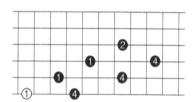
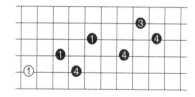
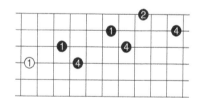

Chord Tones in Scalar Form

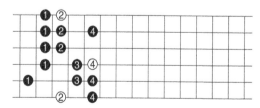
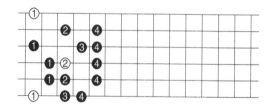

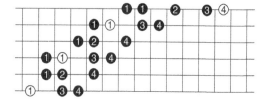
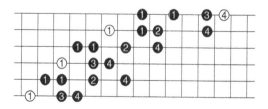

m7♭13

Chord Tones

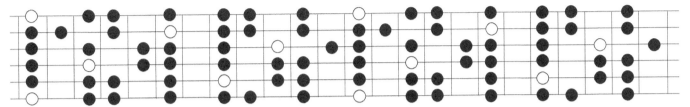

Arpeggio Fingerings

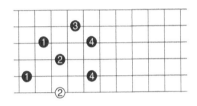 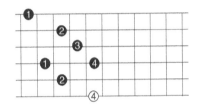 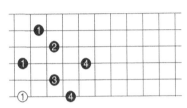

 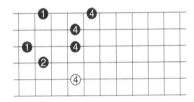 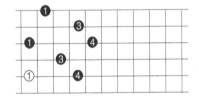

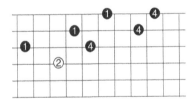 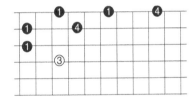 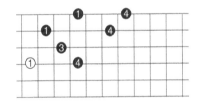

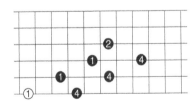 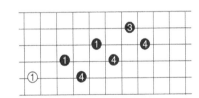 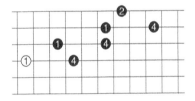

Chord Tones in Scalar Form

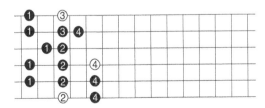 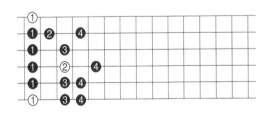

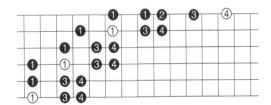 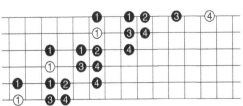

m(maj7)♭13

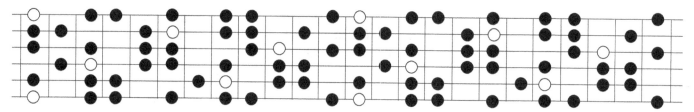

Chord Tones

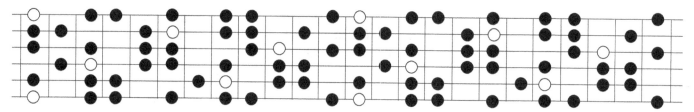

Arpeggio Fingerings

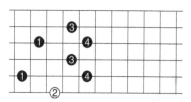
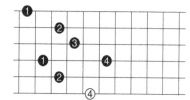
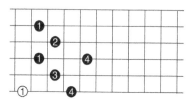

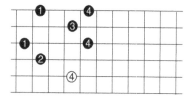
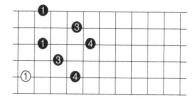

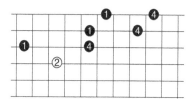
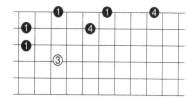
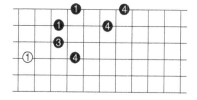

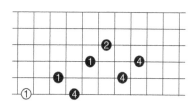
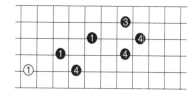
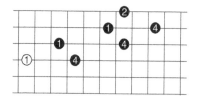

Chord Tones in Scalar Form

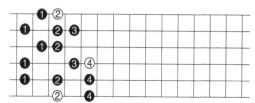
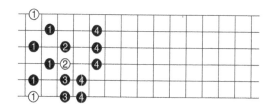

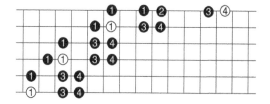
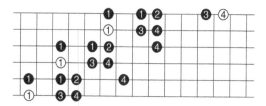

m7♭5♭13

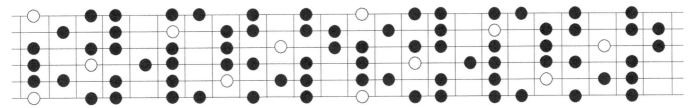

Chord Tones

Arpeggio Fingerings

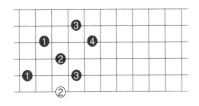
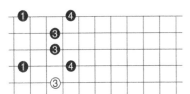
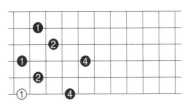

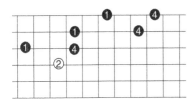
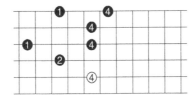
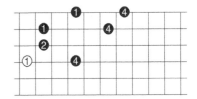

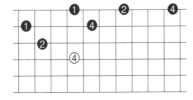
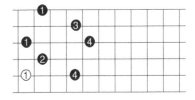
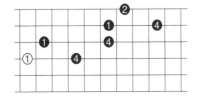

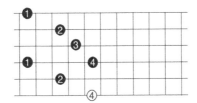

Chord Tones in Scalar Form

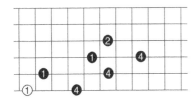
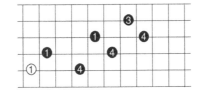

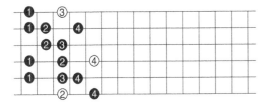
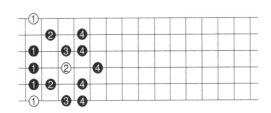

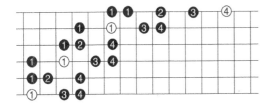
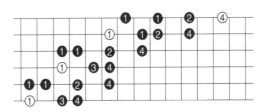

7

Chord Tones

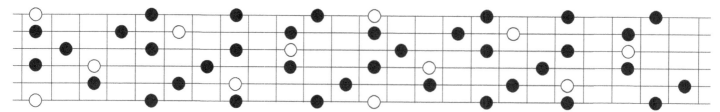

One-Octave Arpeggio Fingerings

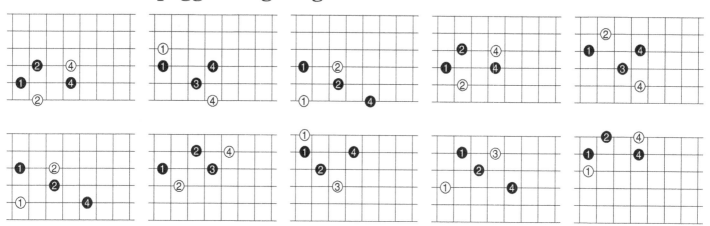

Two-Octave Arpeggio Fingerings

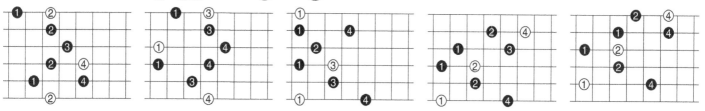

Three-Octave Arpeggio Fingerings

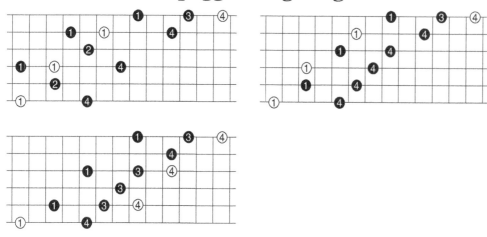

7♭5

Chord Tones

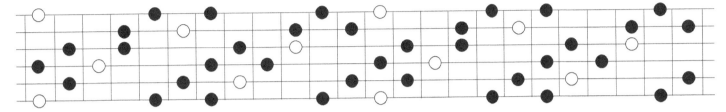

One-Octave Arpeggio Fingerings

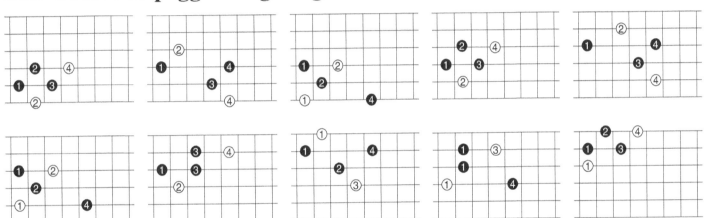

Two-Octave Arpeggio Fingerings

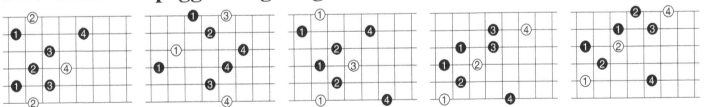

Three-Octave Arpeggio Fingerings

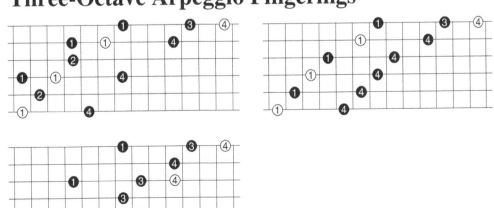

7♯5

Chord Tones

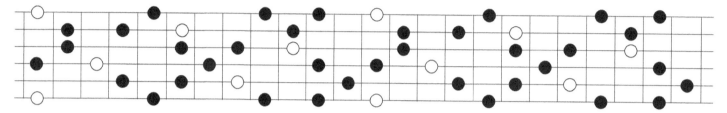

One-Octave Arpeggio Fingerings

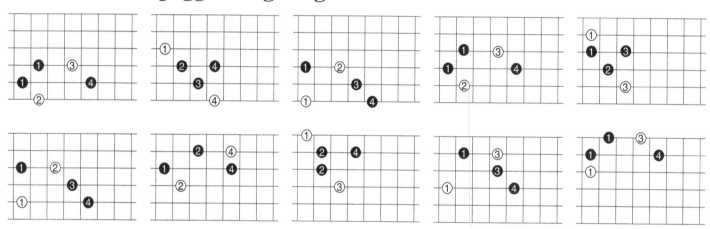

Two-Octave Arpeggio Fingerings

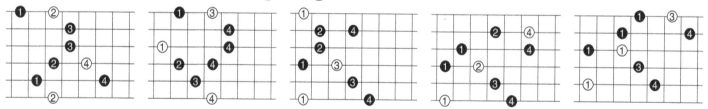

Three-Octave Arpeggio Fingerings

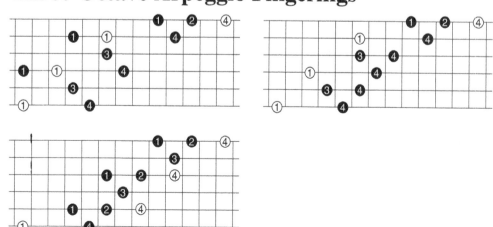

7sus4

Chord Tones

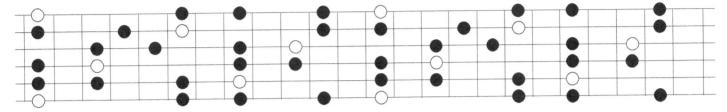

One-Octave Arpeggio Fingerings

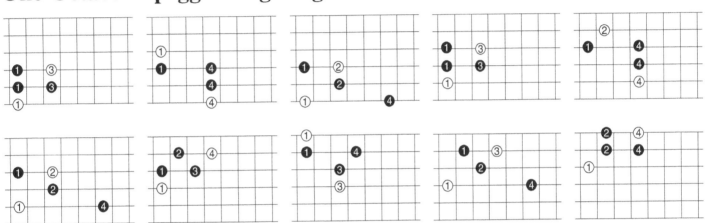

Two-Octave Arpeggio Fingerings

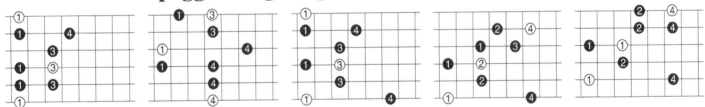

Three-Octave Arpeggio Fingerings

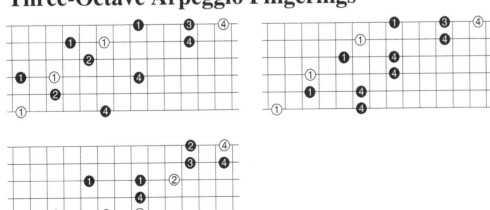

9

Chord Tones

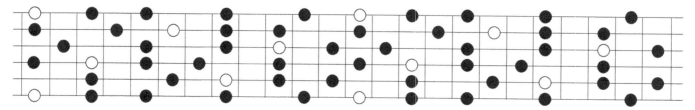

Arpeggio Fingerings

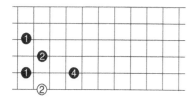
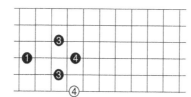
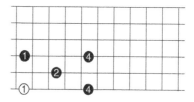

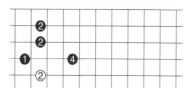
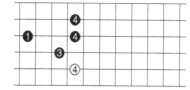
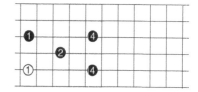

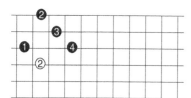
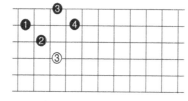
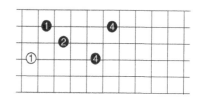

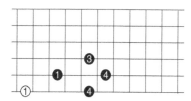
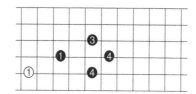
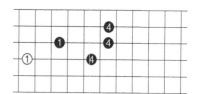

Chord Tones in Scalar Form

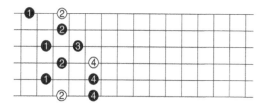
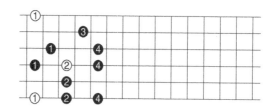

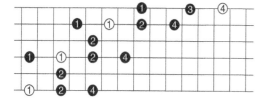
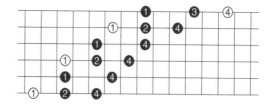

9♭5

Chord Tones

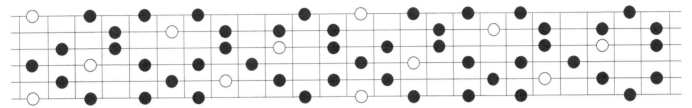

Arpeggio Fingerings

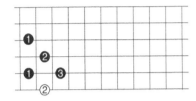 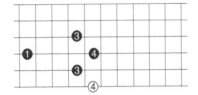 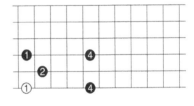

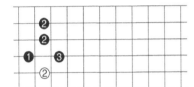 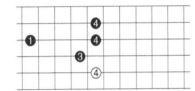 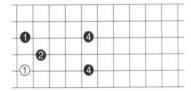

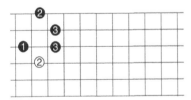 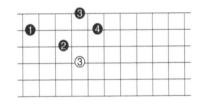 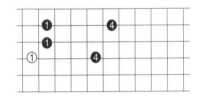

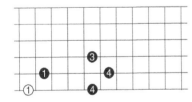  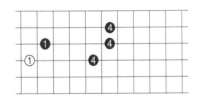

Chord Tones in Scalar Form

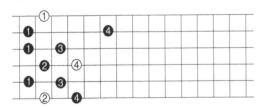 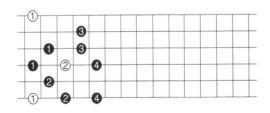

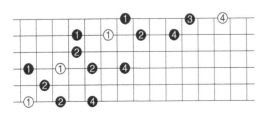 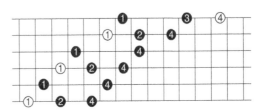

9♯5

Chord Tones

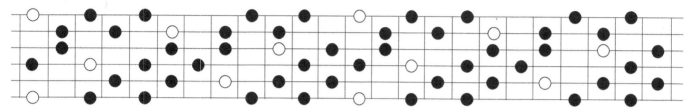

Arpeggio Fingerings

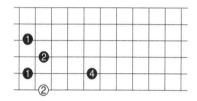
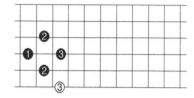
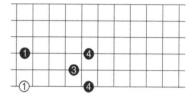

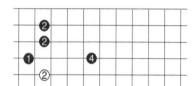

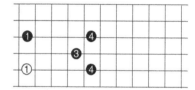

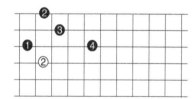
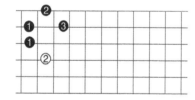
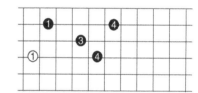

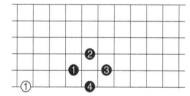
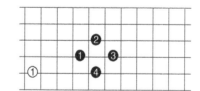
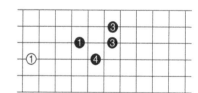

Chord Tones in Scalar Form

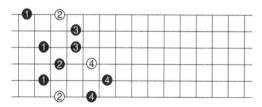
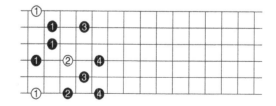

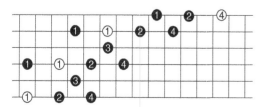
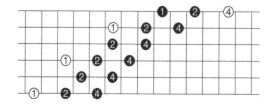

9♯11

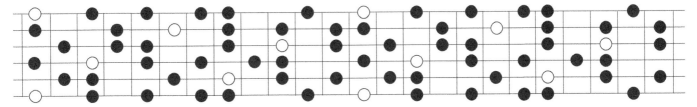

Chord Tones

Arpeggio Fingerings

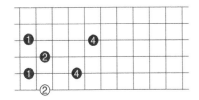
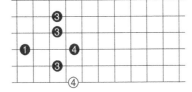
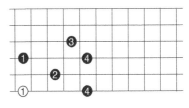

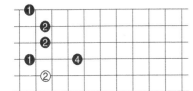
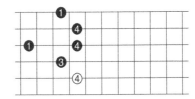
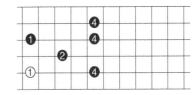

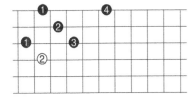
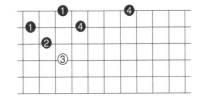
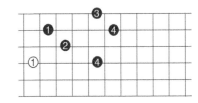

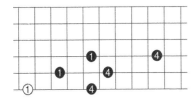
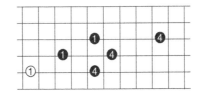
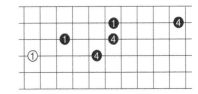

Chord Tones in Scalar Form

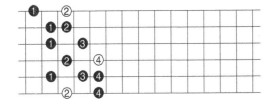
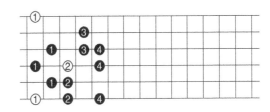

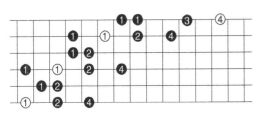
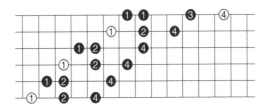

9♯5♯11

Chord Tones

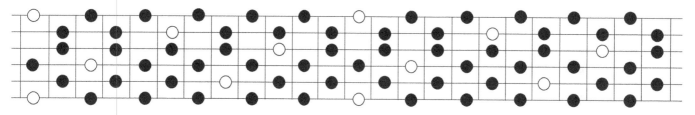

Arpeggio Fingerings

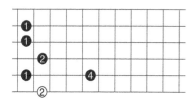 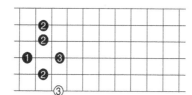 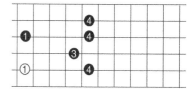

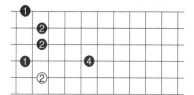 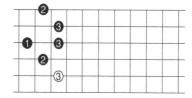 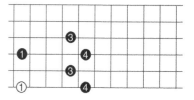

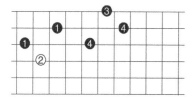 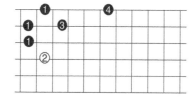 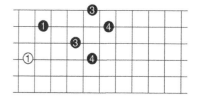

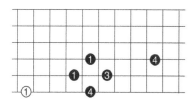 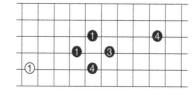 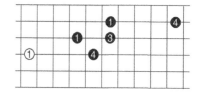

Chord Tones in Scalar Form

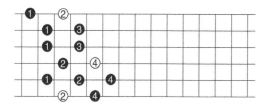 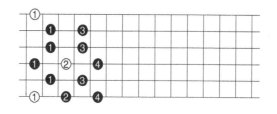

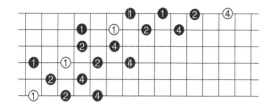 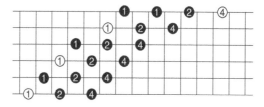

9sus4

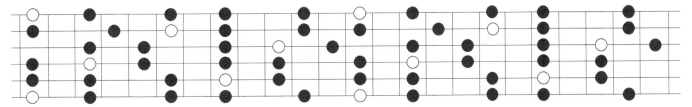

Chord Tones

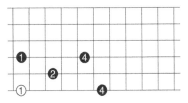

Arpeggio Fingerings

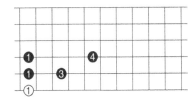
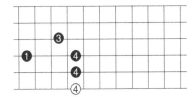
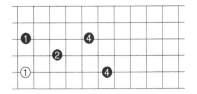

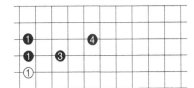
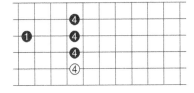

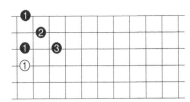
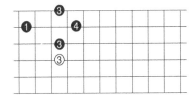
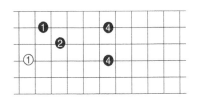

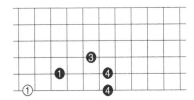
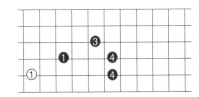
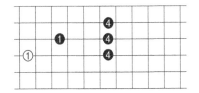

Chord Tones in Scalar Form

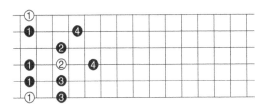
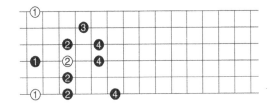

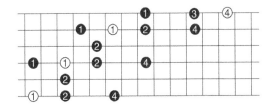
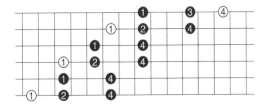

11

Chord Tones

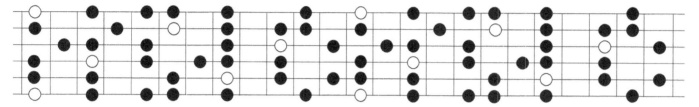

Arpeggio Fingerings

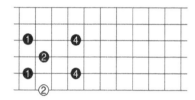
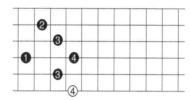
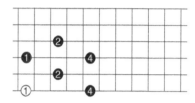

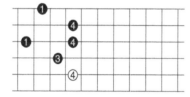
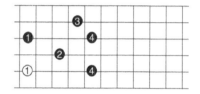

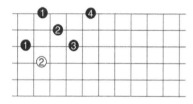
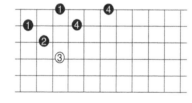
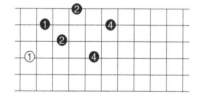

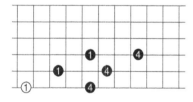
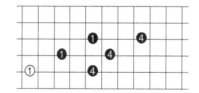
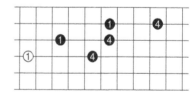

Chord Tones in Scalar Form

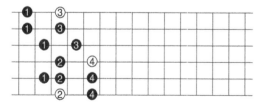
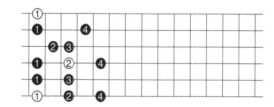

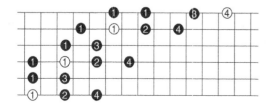
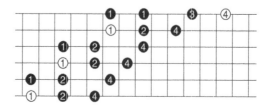

13

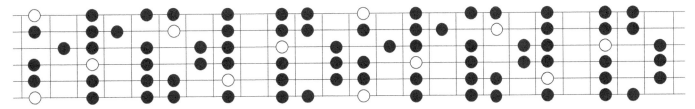

Chord Tones

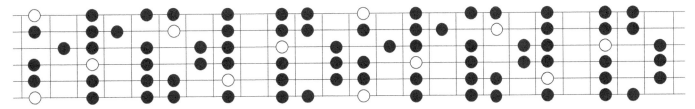

Arpeggio Fingerings

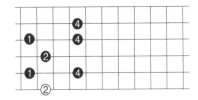
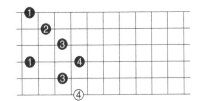
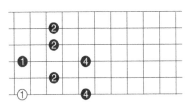

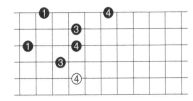
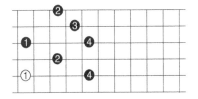

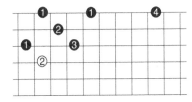
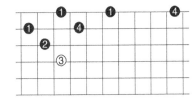
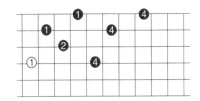

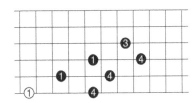
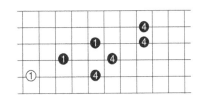
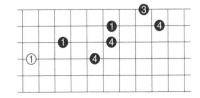

Chord Tones in Scalar Form

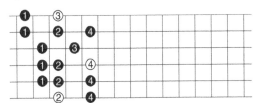
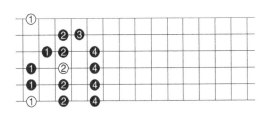

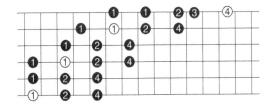
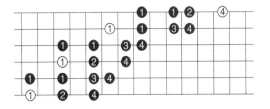

13♯11

Chord Tones

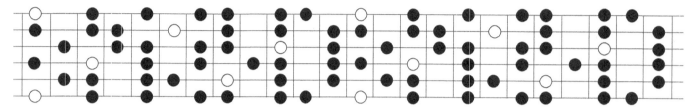

Arpeggio Fingerings

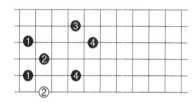
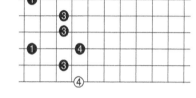
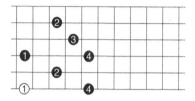

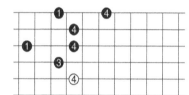
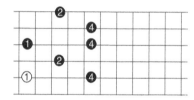

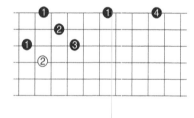
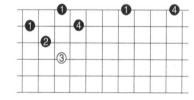
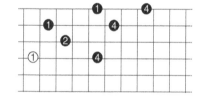

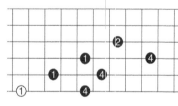
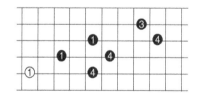
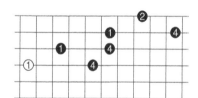

Chord Tones in Scalar Form

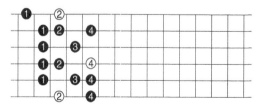
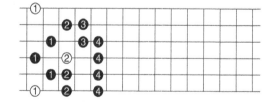

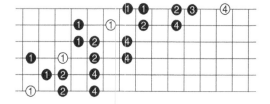
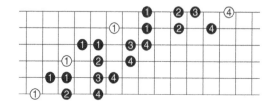

13sus4

Chord Tones

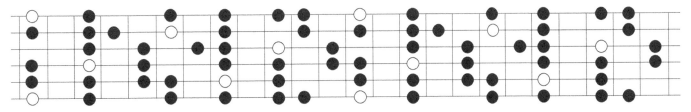

Arpeggio Fingerings

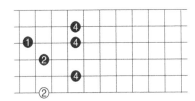
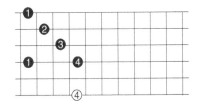
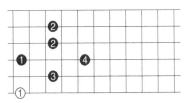

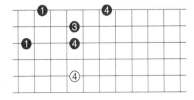
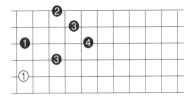

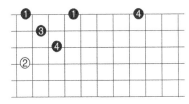
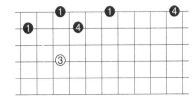
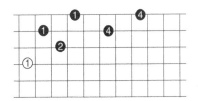

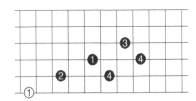
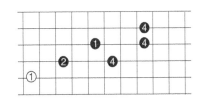
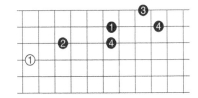

Chord Tones in Scalar Form

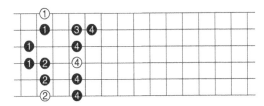
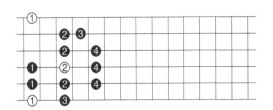

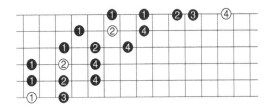
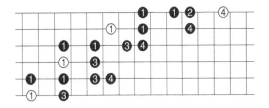

7♭9

Chord Tones

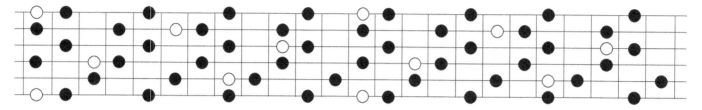

Arpeggio Fingerings

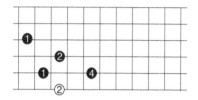
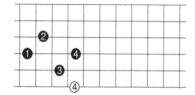
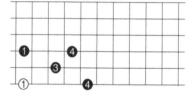

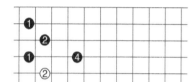

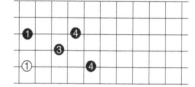

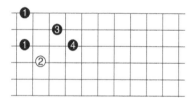
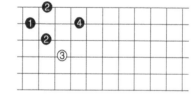
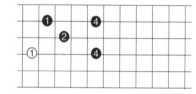

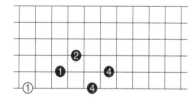
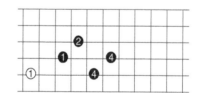
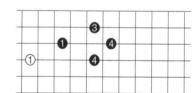

Chord Tones in Scalar Form

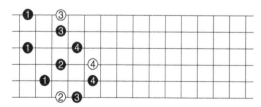
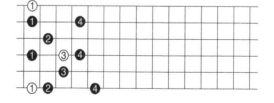

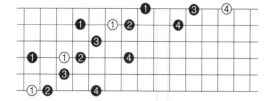
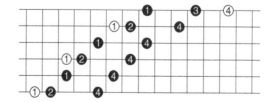

7♯9

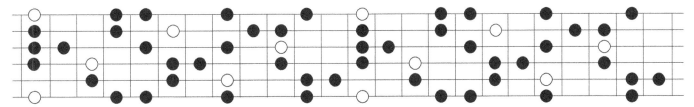

Chord Tones

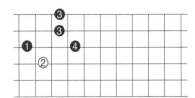

Arpeggio Fingerings

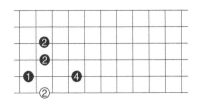 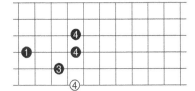 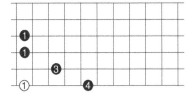

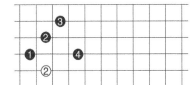 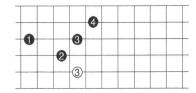 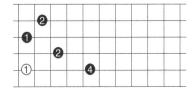

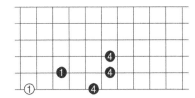 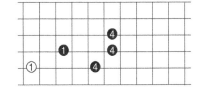 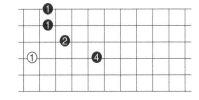

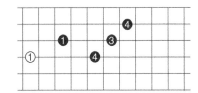

Chord Tones in Scalar Form

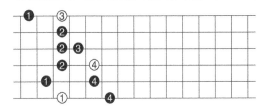 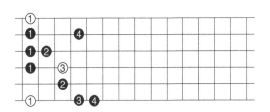

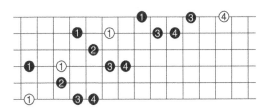 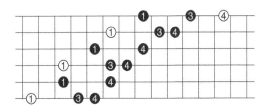

7♭9♯9

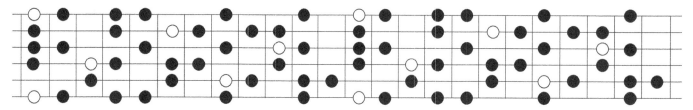

Chord Tones

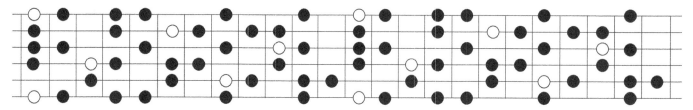

Arpeggio Fingerings

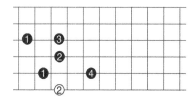
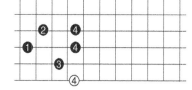
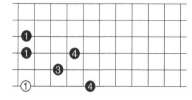

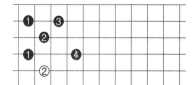
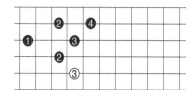
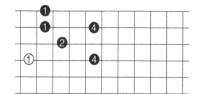

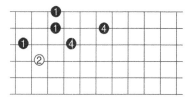
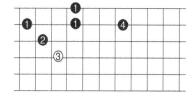
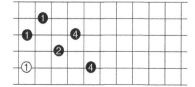

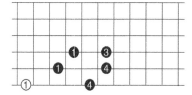

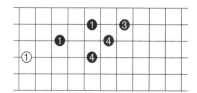

Chord Tones in Scalar Form

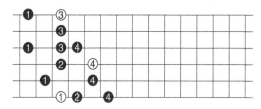
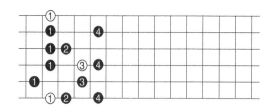

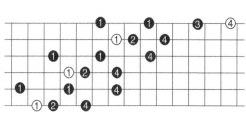
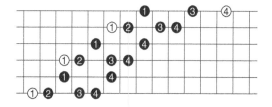

7♭9♭5

Chord Tones

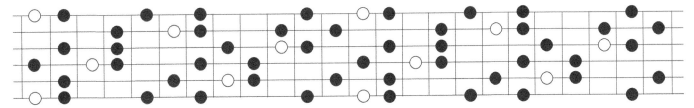

Arpeggio Fingerings

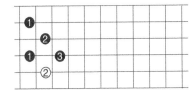
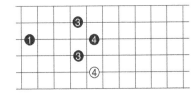
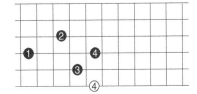

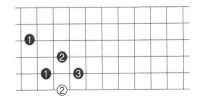
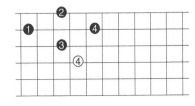
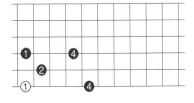

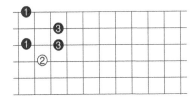
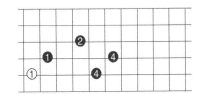
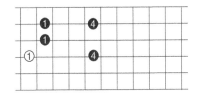

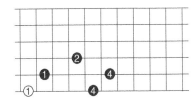
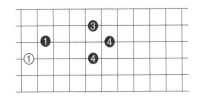
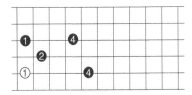

Chord Tones in Scalar Form

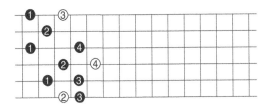
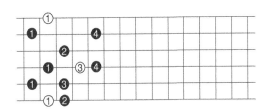

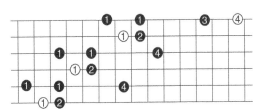
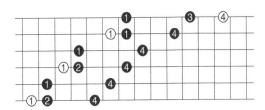

7#9♭5

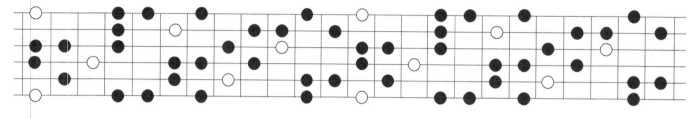

Chord Tones

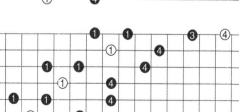

Arpeggio Fingerings

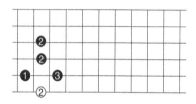
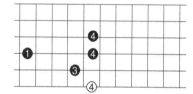
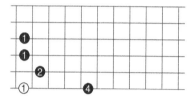

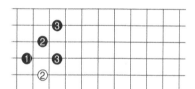
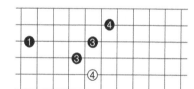
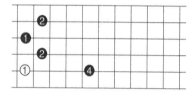

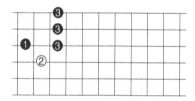
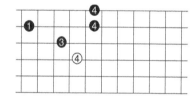
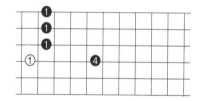

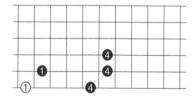
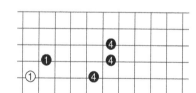
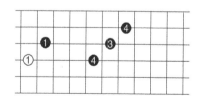

Chord Tones in Scalar Form

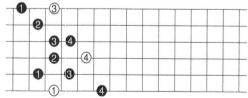
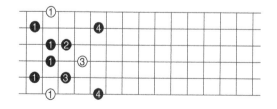

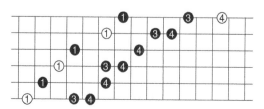

7♭9♯9♭5

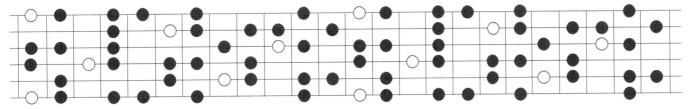

Chord Tones

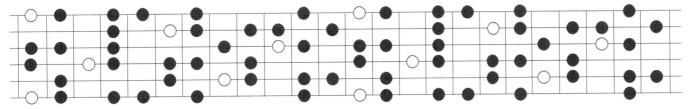

Arpeggio Fingerings

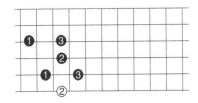
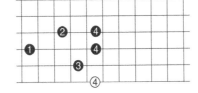
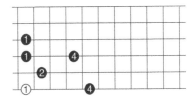

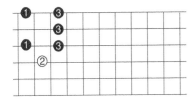
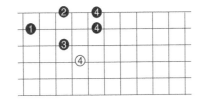
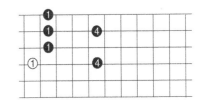

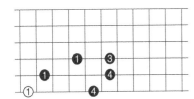
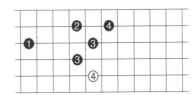
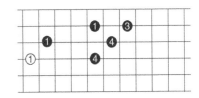

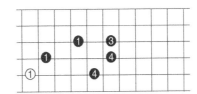
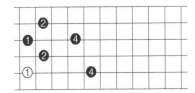

Chord Tones in Scalar Form

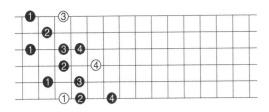
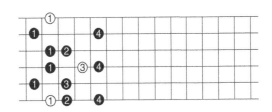

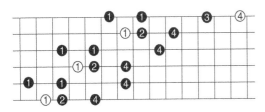
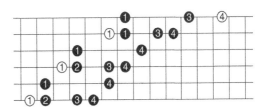

7♭9♯5

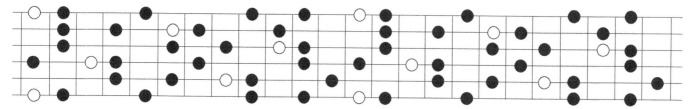

Chord Tones

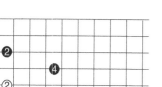

Arpeggio Fingerings

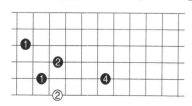
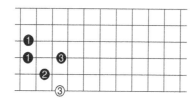
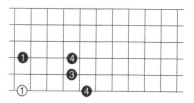

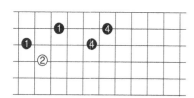
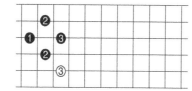
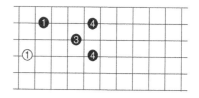

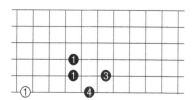
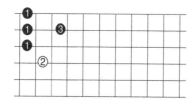
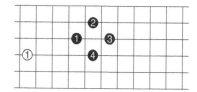

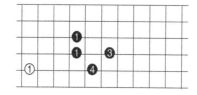
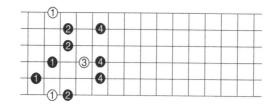

Chord Tones in Scalar Form

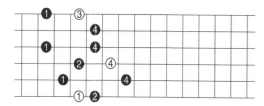
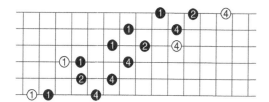
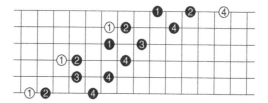

7♯9♯5

Chord Tones

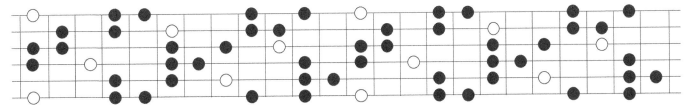

Arpeggio Fingerings

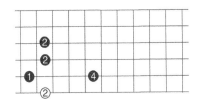 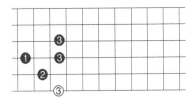 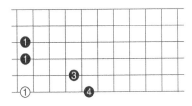

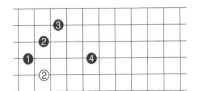 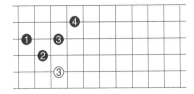 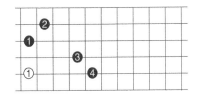

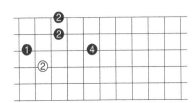 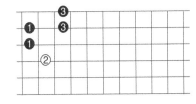 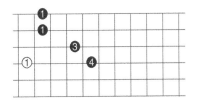

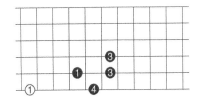 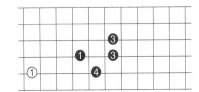 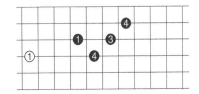

Chord Tones in Scalar Form

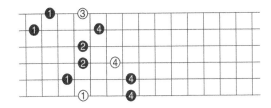 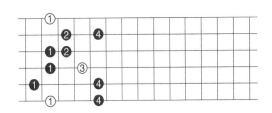

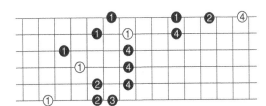 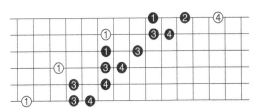

7♭9♯9♯5

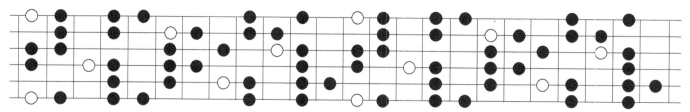

Chord Tones

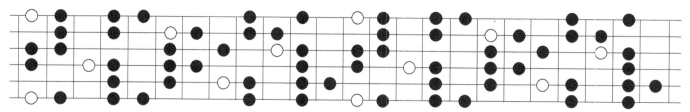

Arpeggio Fingerings

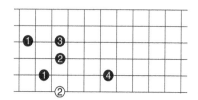 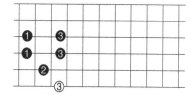 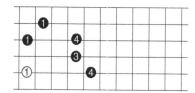

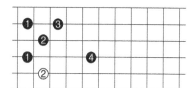 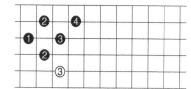 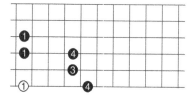

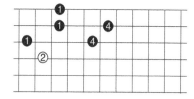 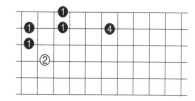 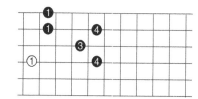

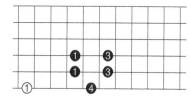 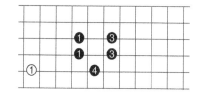 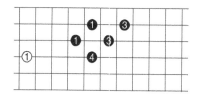

Chord Tones in Scalar Form

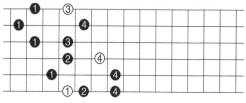 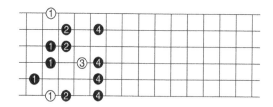

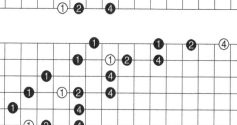 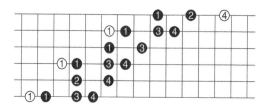

7sus4♭9

Chord Tones

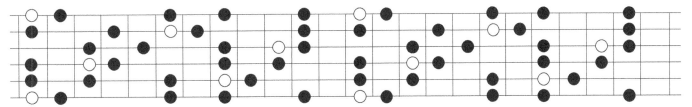

Arpeggio Fingerings

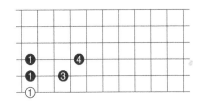
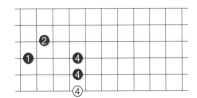
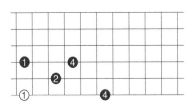

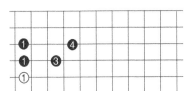
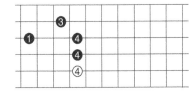
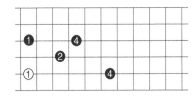

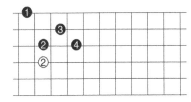
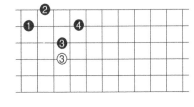
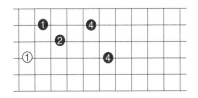

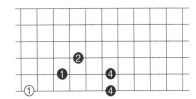
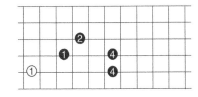
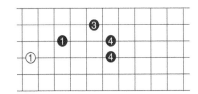

Chord Tones in Scalar Form

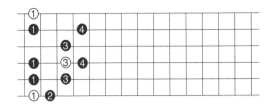
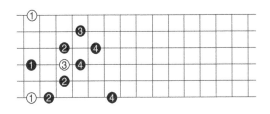

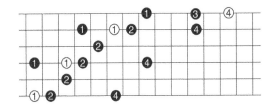
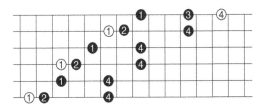

11♭9

Chord Tones

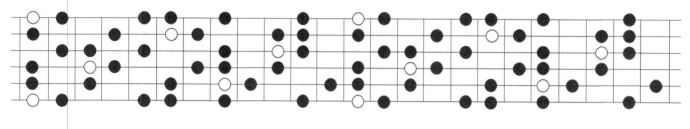

Arpeggio Fingerings

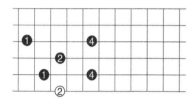 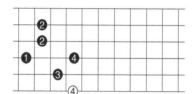 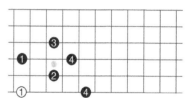

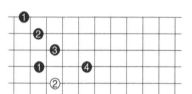 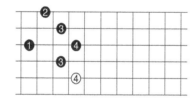 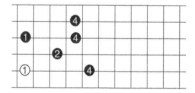

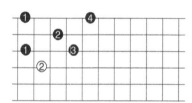 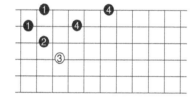 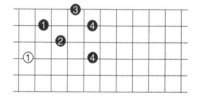

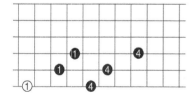 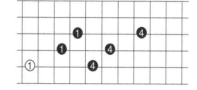 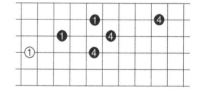

Chord Tones in Scalar Form

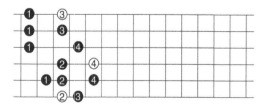 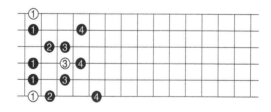

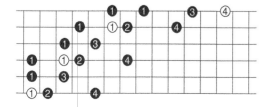 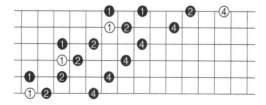

7♭9♯11

Chord Tones

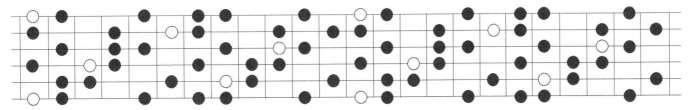

Arpeggio Fingerings

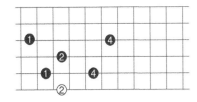
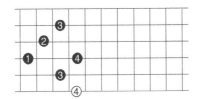
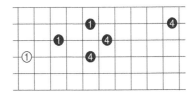

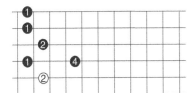
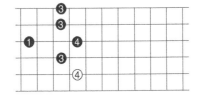
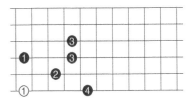

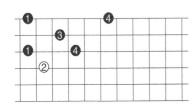
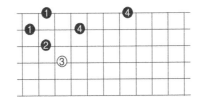
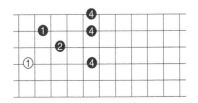

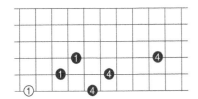
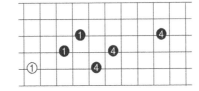
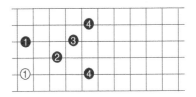

Chord Tones in Scalar Form

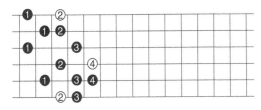
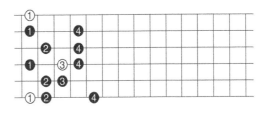

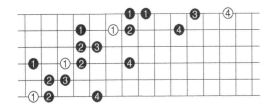
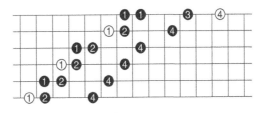

7♯9♯11

Chord Tones

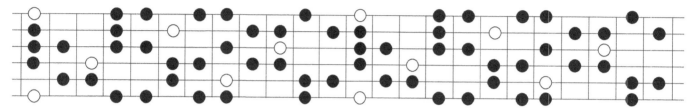

Arpeggio Fingerings

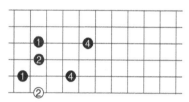
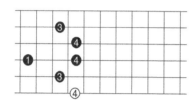
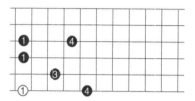

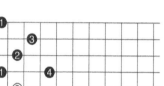
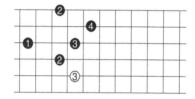
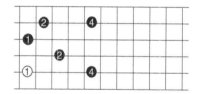

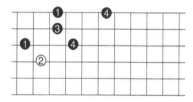
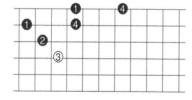
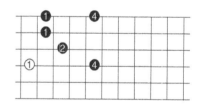

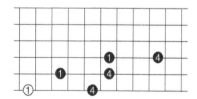
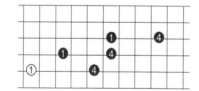
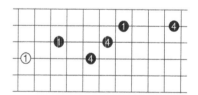

Chord Tones in Scalar Form

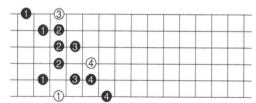
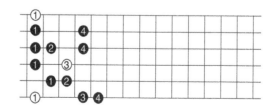

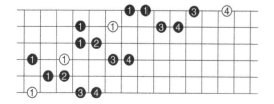
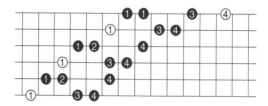

7♭9♯9♯11

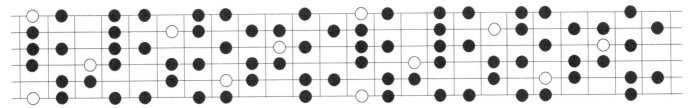

Chord Tones

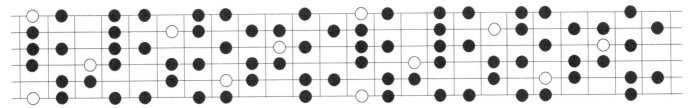

Arpeggio Fingerings

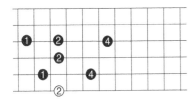 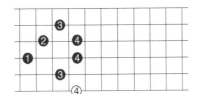 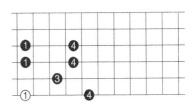

 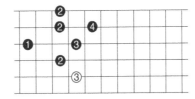 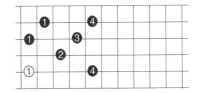

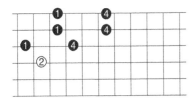 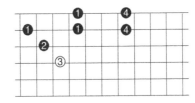 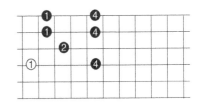

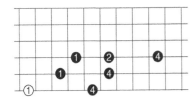 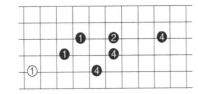 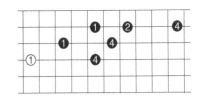

Chord Tones in Scalar Form

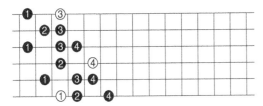 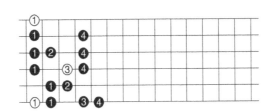

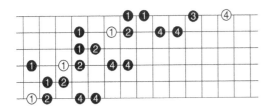 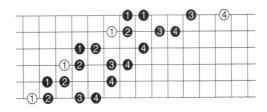

7♭9♯5♯11

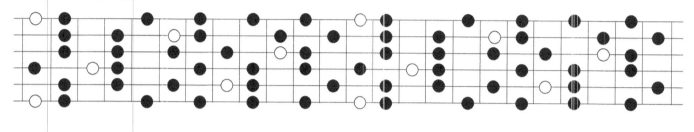

Chord Tones

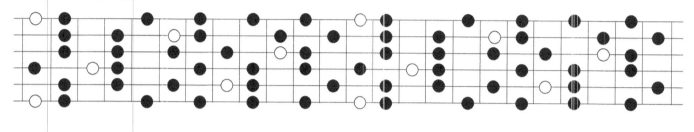

Arpeggio Fingerings

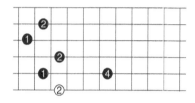
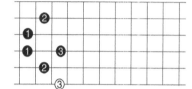
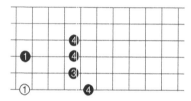

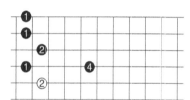

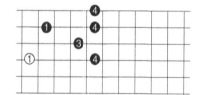

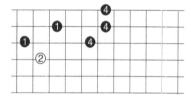
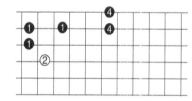
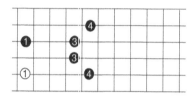

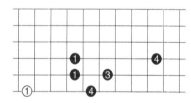
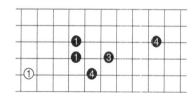
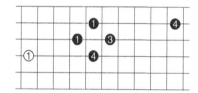

Chord Tones in Scalar Form

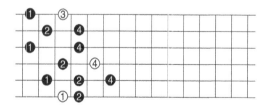
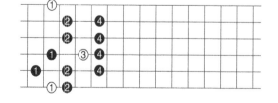

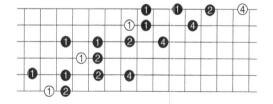
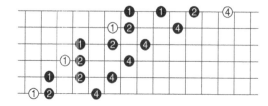

7♯9♯5♯11

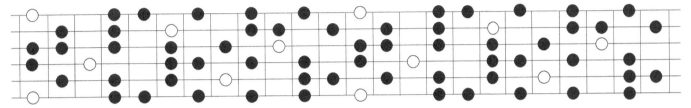

Chord Tones

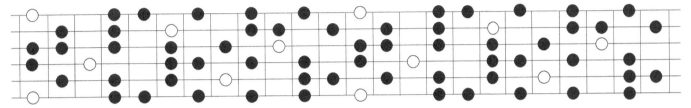

Arpeggio Fingerings

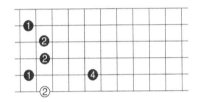
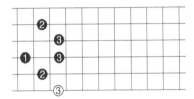
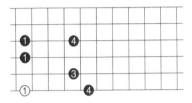

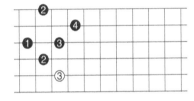
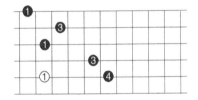

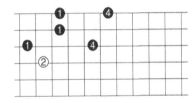
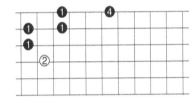
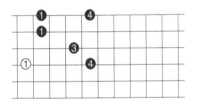

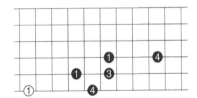
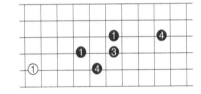
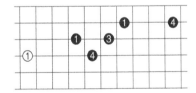

Chord Tones in Scalar Form

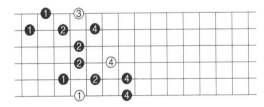
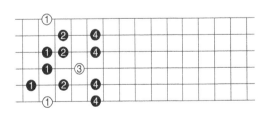

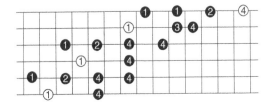
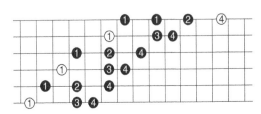

7♭9♯9♯5♯11

Chord Tones

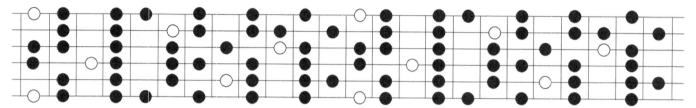

Arpeggio Fingerings

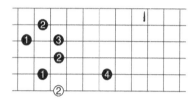
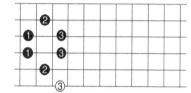
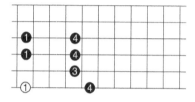

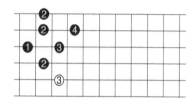
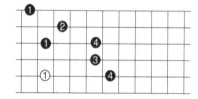

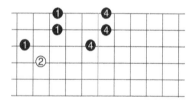
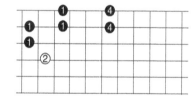
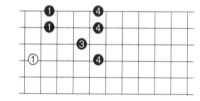

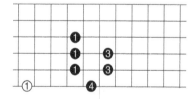

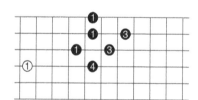

Chord Tones in Scalar Form

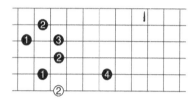

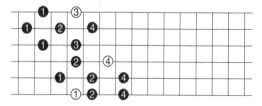
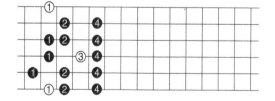

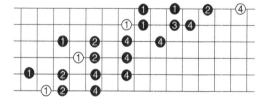
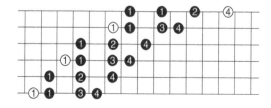

13♭9

Chord Tones

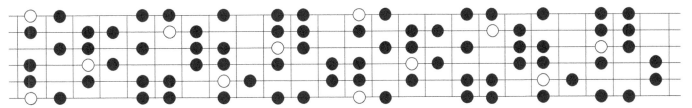

Arpeggio Fingerings

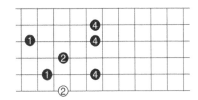
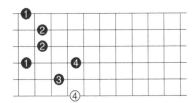
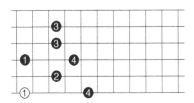

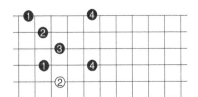
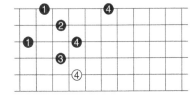
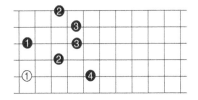

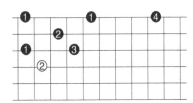
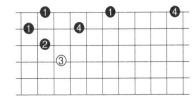
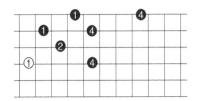

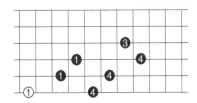
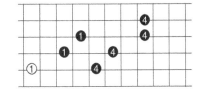
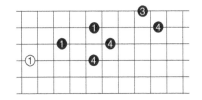

Chord Tones in Scalar Form

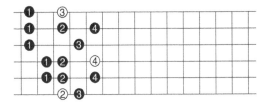
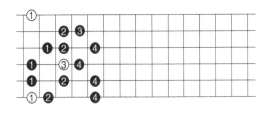

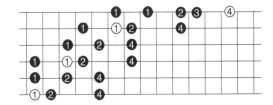
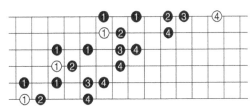

13sus4♭9

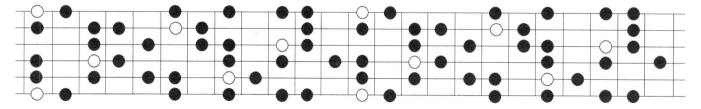

Chord Tones

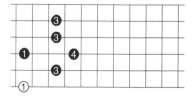

Arpeggio Fingerings

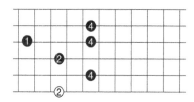
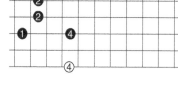
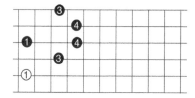

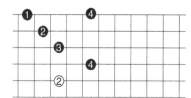
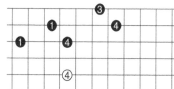
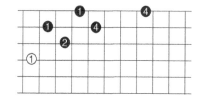

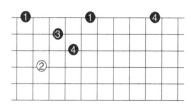
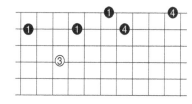
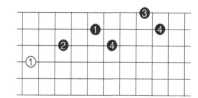

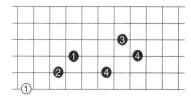
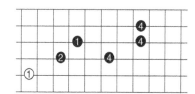

Chord Tones in Scalar Form

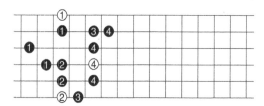
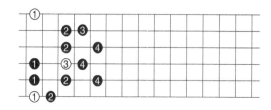

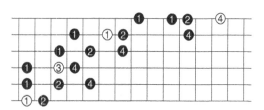
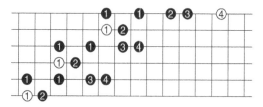

13♭9♯11

Chord Tones

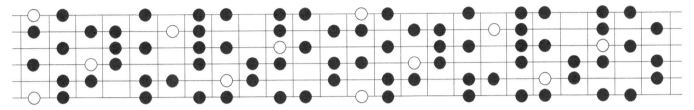

Arpeggio Fingerings

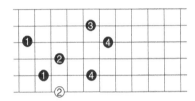
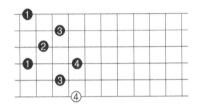
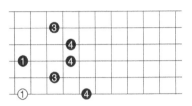

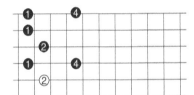
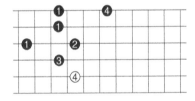
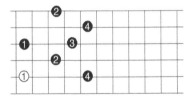

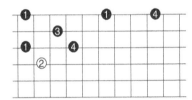
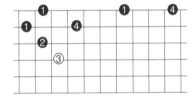
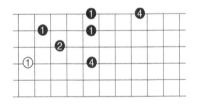

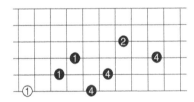
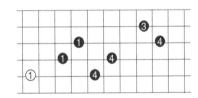
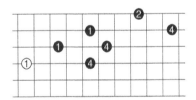

Chord Tones in Scalar Form

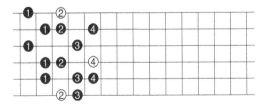
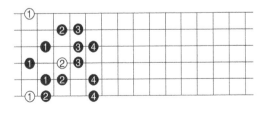

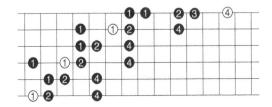
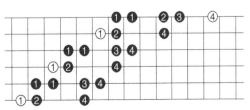

13♯9♯11

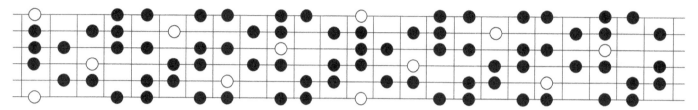

Chord Tones

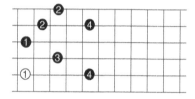

Arpeggio Fingerings

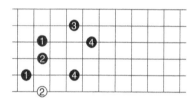
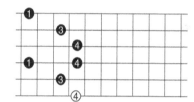
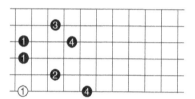

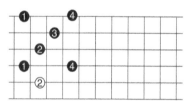
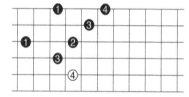
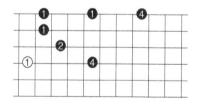

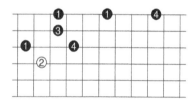
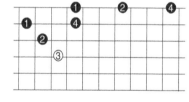
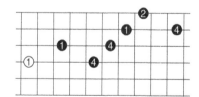

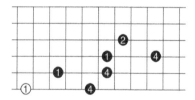
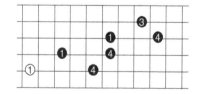

Chord Tones in Scalar Form

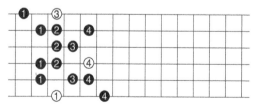
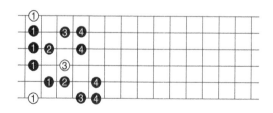

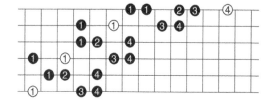
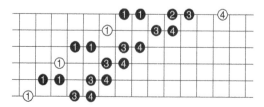

13♭9♯9♯11

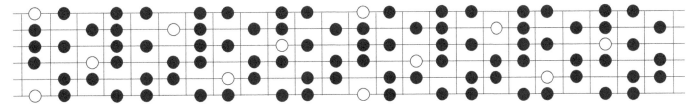

Chord Tones

Arpeggio Fingerings

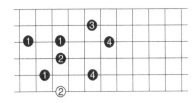
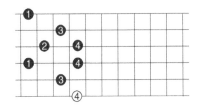
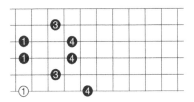

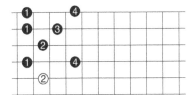
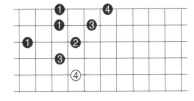
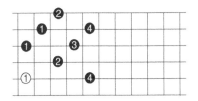

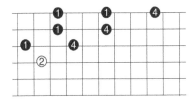
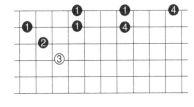
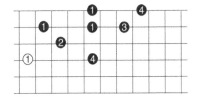

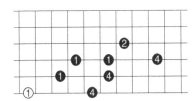
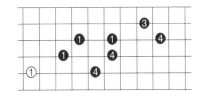
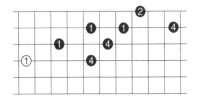

Chord Tones in Scalar Form

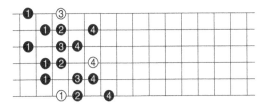
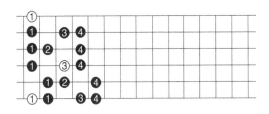

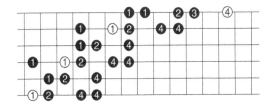
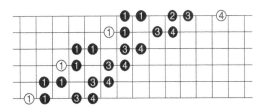

7♭13

Chord Tones

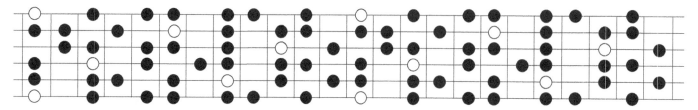

Arpeggio Fingerings

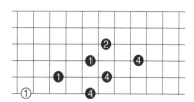
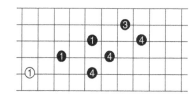
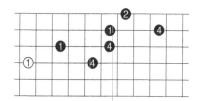

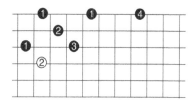
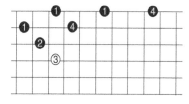
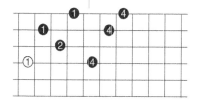

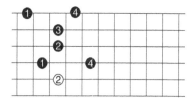
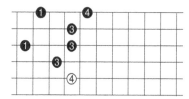
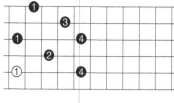

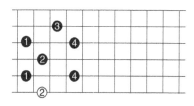
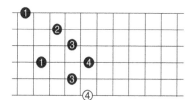
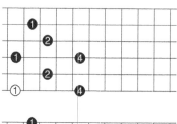

Chord Tones in Scalar Form

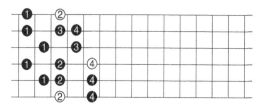
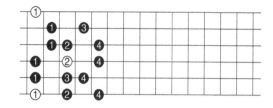

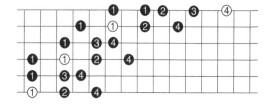
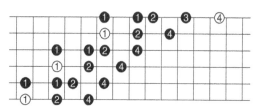

7sus4♭9♭13

Chord Tones

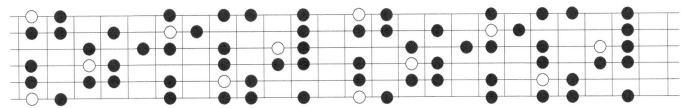

Arpeggio Fingerings

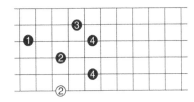
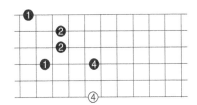
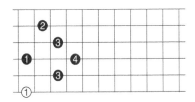

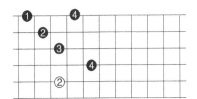
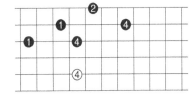
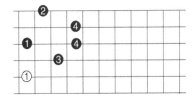

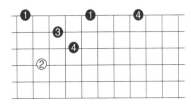
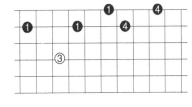
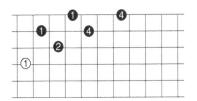

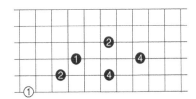
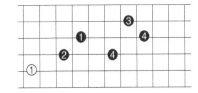
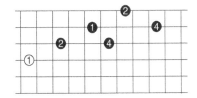

Chord Tones in Scalar Form

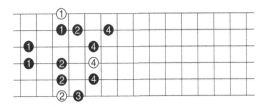
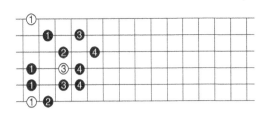

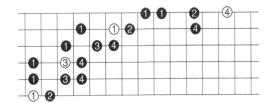
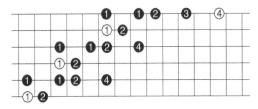

7♭9♭13♭5

Chord Tones

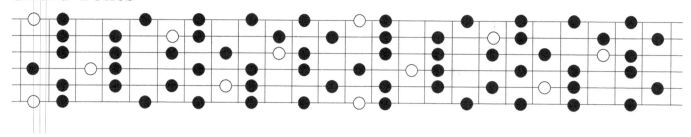

Arpeggio Fingerings

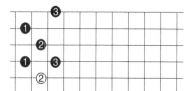
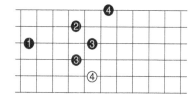
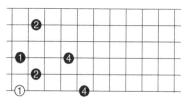

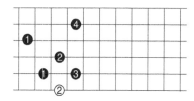
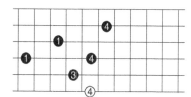
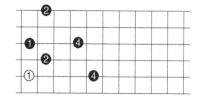

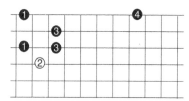
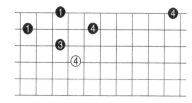
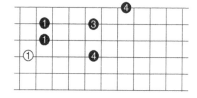

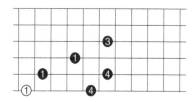
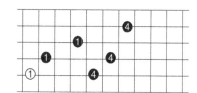
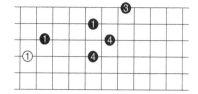

Chord Tones in Scalar Form

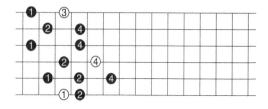
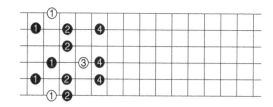

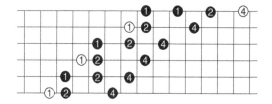
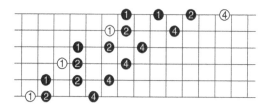

7♯9♭13♭5

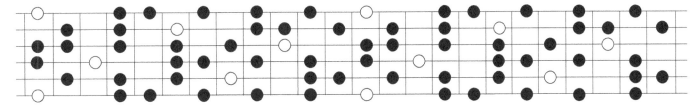

Chord Tones

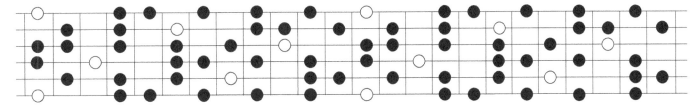

Arpeggio Fingerings

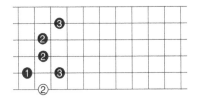
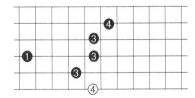
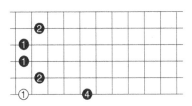

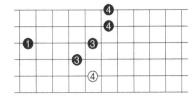
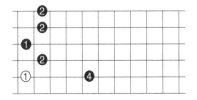

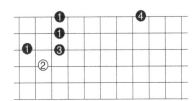
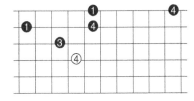
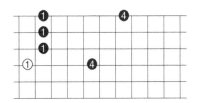

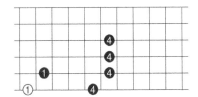
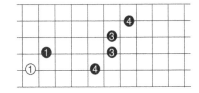
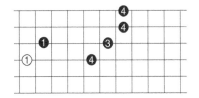

Chord Tones in Scalar Form

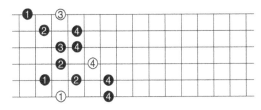
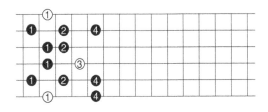

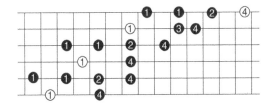
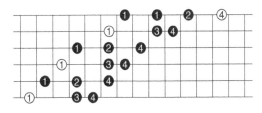

7♭9♯9♭13♭5

Chord Tones

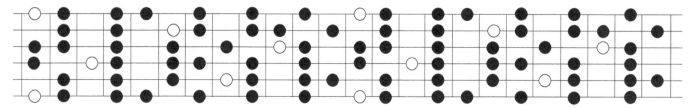

Arpeggio Fingerings

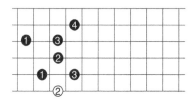
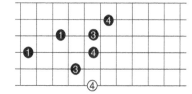
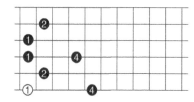

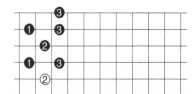
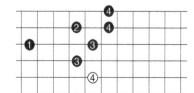
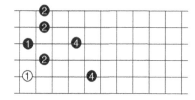

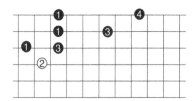
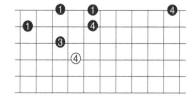
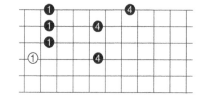

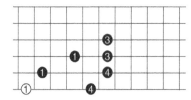

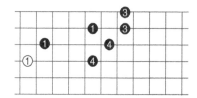

Chord Tones in Scalar Form

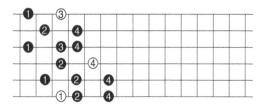
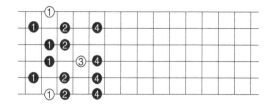

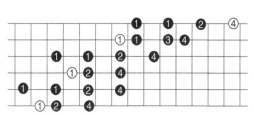
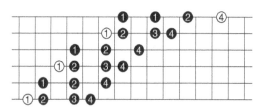

P4+P4

Chord Tones

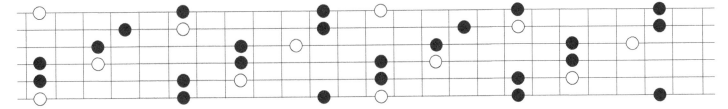

One-Octave Arpeggio Fingerings

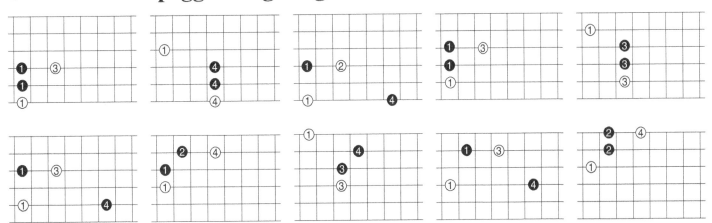

Two-Octave Arpeggio Fingerings

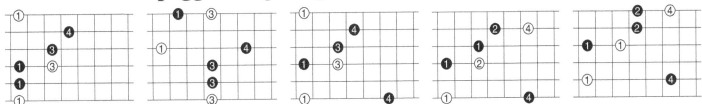

Three-Octave Arpeggio Fingerings

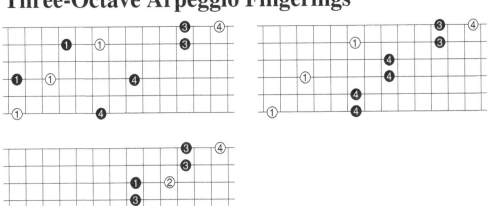

P4+A4

Chord Tones

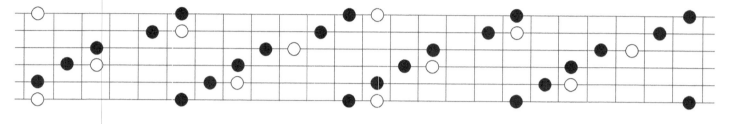

One-Octave Arpeggio Fingerings

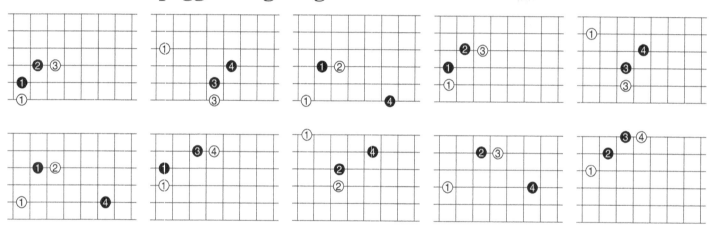

Two-Octave Arpeggio Fingerings

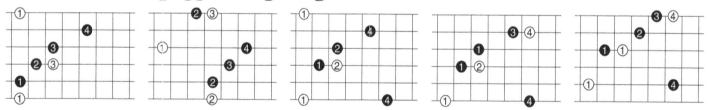

Three-Octave Arpeggio Fingerings

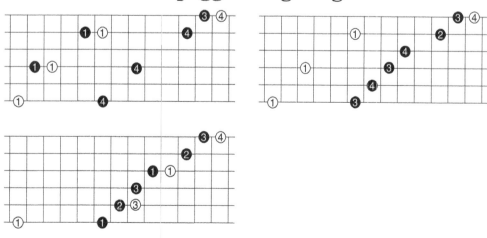

A4+P4

Chord Tones

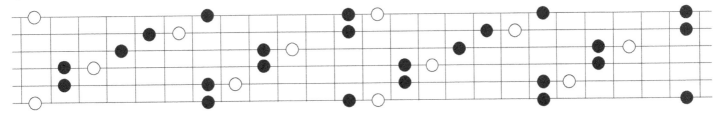

One-Octave Arpeggio Fingerings

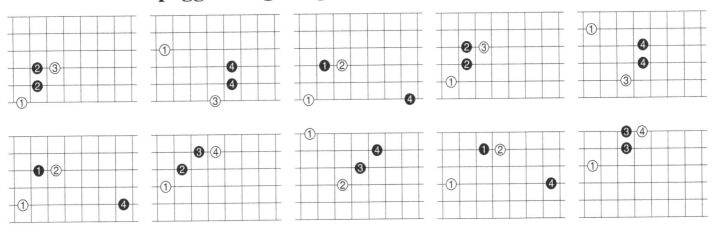

Two-Octave Arpeggio Fingerings

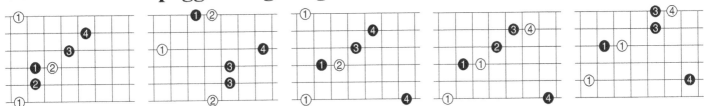

Three-Octave Arpeggio Fingerings

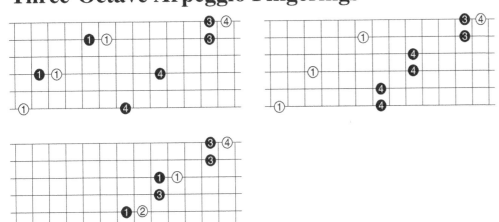

P4+P4+P4

Chord Tones

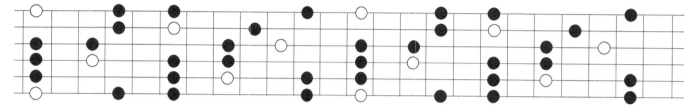

Arpeggio Fingerings

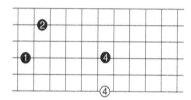
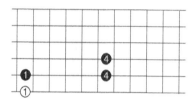

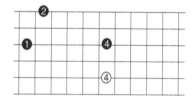
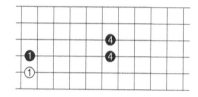

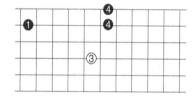
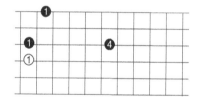

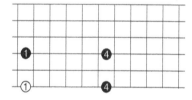
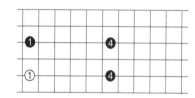
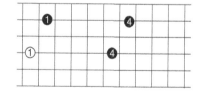

Chord Tones in Scalar Form

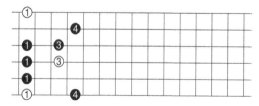
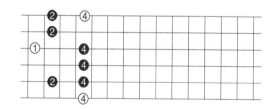

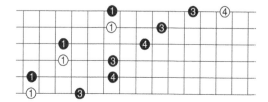
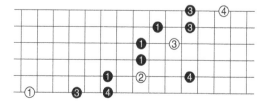

P4+P4+A4

Chord Tones

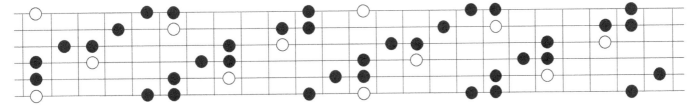

Arpeggio Fingerings

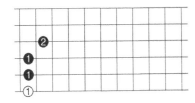
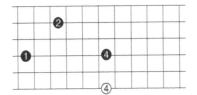
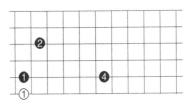

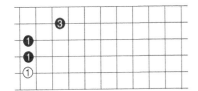
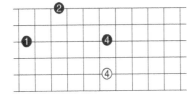
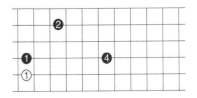

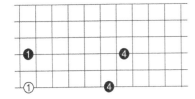
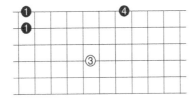
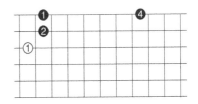

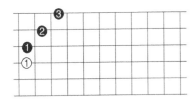
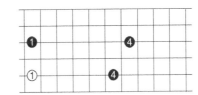
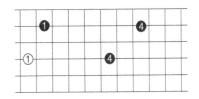

Chord Tones in Scalar Form

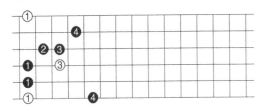
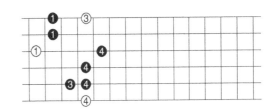

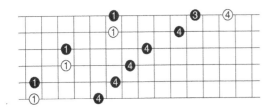
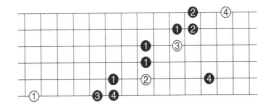

P4+A4+P4

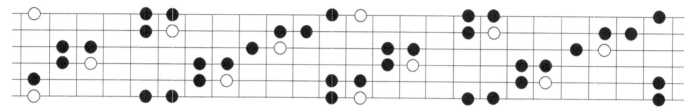

Chord Tones

Arpeggio Fingerings

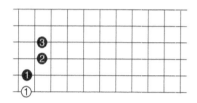
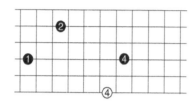
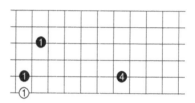

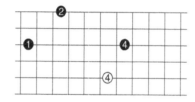
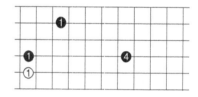

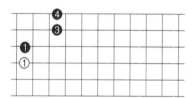
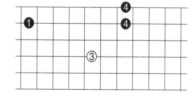
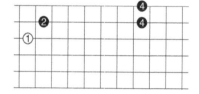

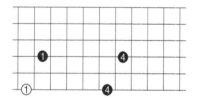
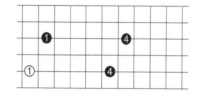
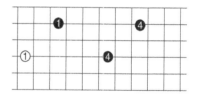

Chord Tones in Scalar Form

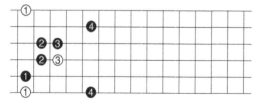
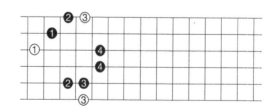

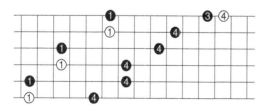
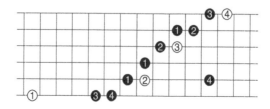

A4+P4+P4

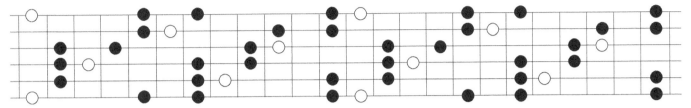

Chord Tones

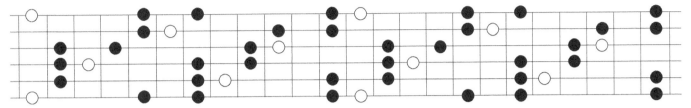

Arpeggio Fingerings

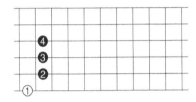
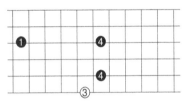

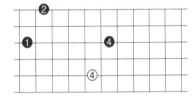
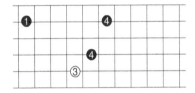

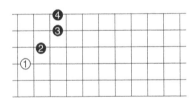
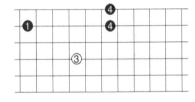
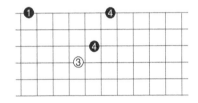

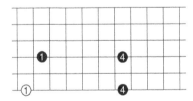
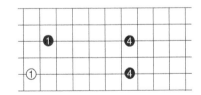
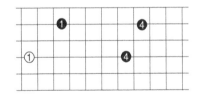

Chord Tones in Scalar Form

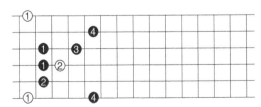
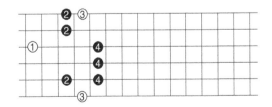

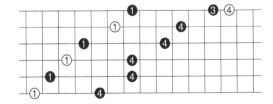
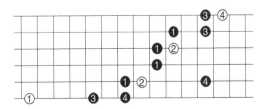

P5+P5

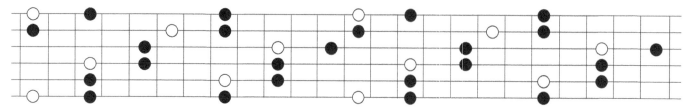

Chord Tones

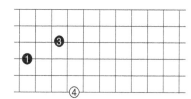
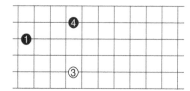
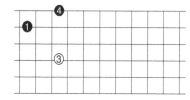

Arpeggio Fingerings

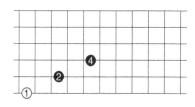
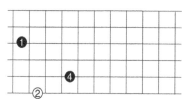

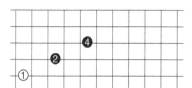
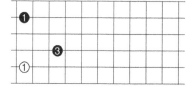

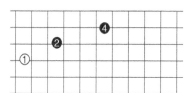
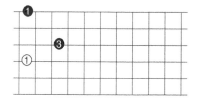

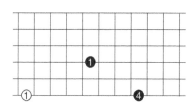
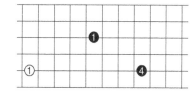
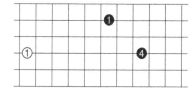

Chord Tones in Scalar Form

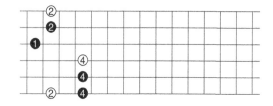
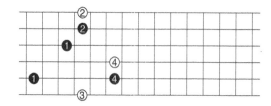

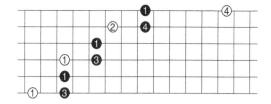
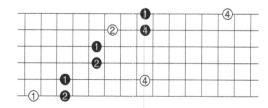

P5+P5+P5

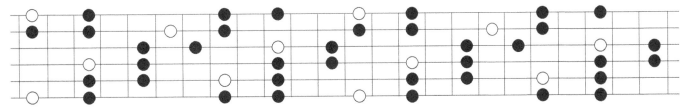

Chord Tones

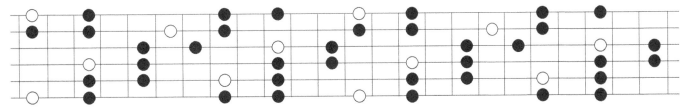

Arpeggio Fingerings

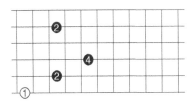
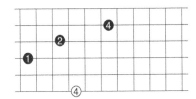
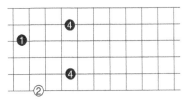

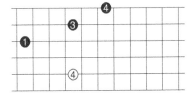
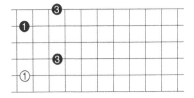

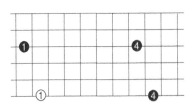
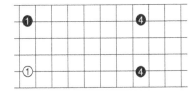
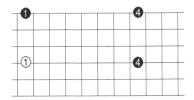

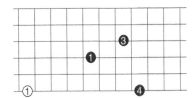
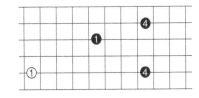
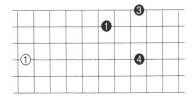

Chord Tones in Scalar Form

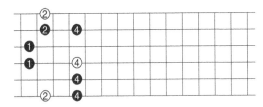
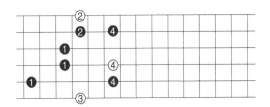

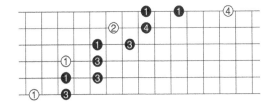
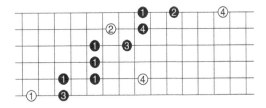

The Arpeggios

Major

1 3 5

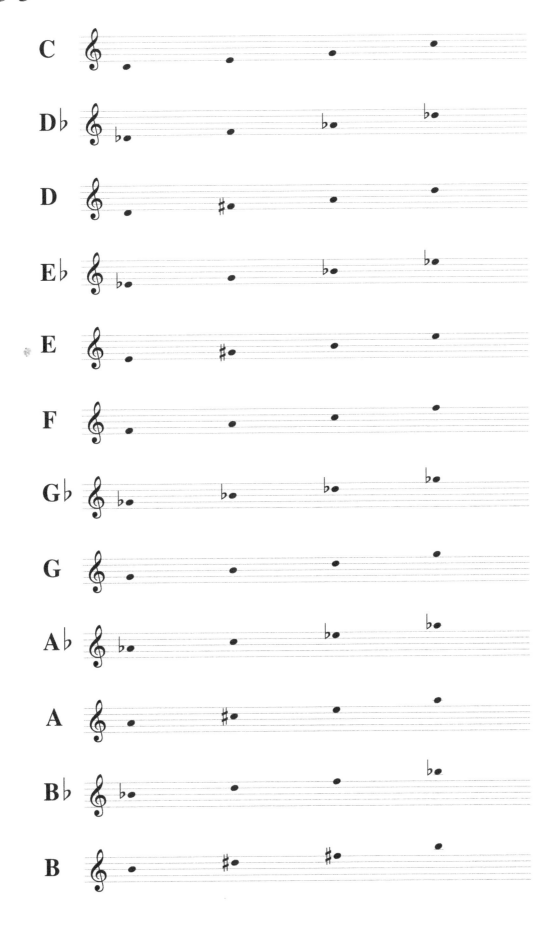

Minor

1 ♭3 5

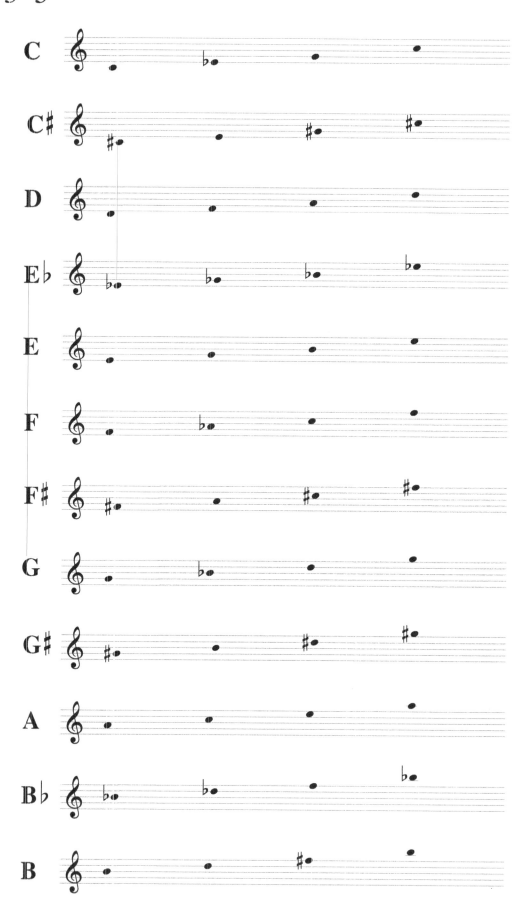

Augmented

1 3 ♯5

Diminished

1 ♭3 ♭5

sus4

1 4 5

sus2

1 2 5

add9

1 3 5 9

madd9

1 ♭3 5 9

6

1 3 5 6

m6

1 ♭3 5 6

6/9

1 3 5 6 9

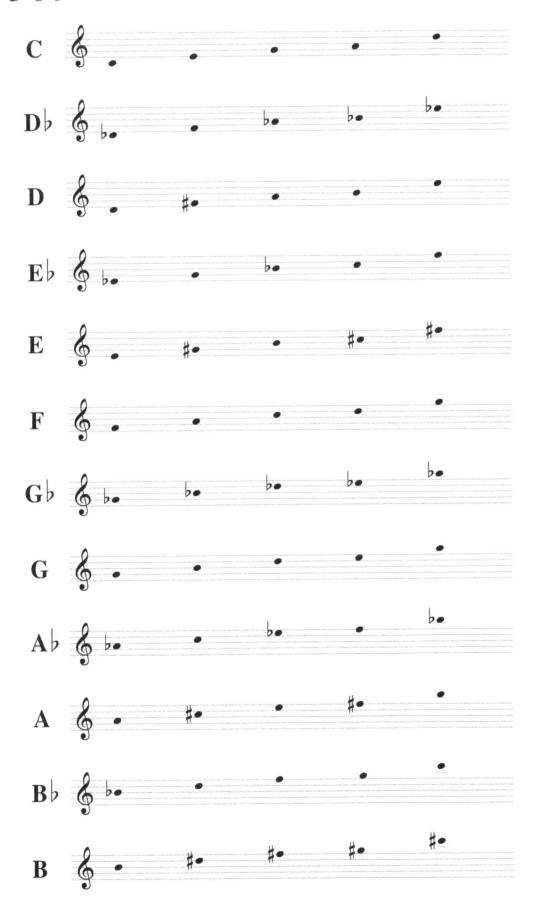

m6/9

1 ♭3 5 6 9

dim7

1 ♭3 ♭5 ♭♭7

maj7

1 3 5 7

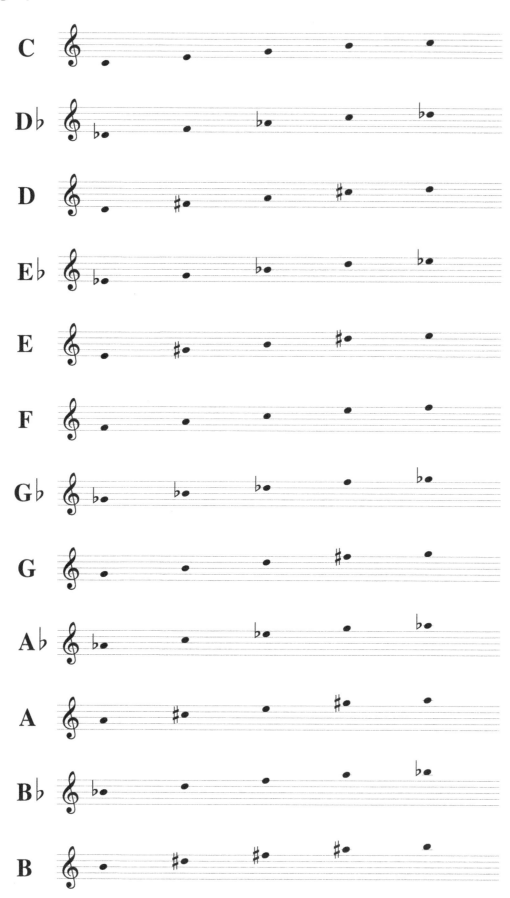

maj7♭5

1 3 ♭5 7

maj7♯5

1 3 ♯5 7

maj7♭6

1 3 5 ♭6 7

maj9

13 5 7 9

maj9♭5

13 ♭5 7 9

maj9♯5

1 3 ♯5 7 9

maj9♯11

1 3 5 7 9 ♯11

maj9♯11♯5

1 3 ♯5 7 9 ♯11

maj9♭6

1 3 5 ♭6 7 9

maj7#9

1 3 5 7 #9

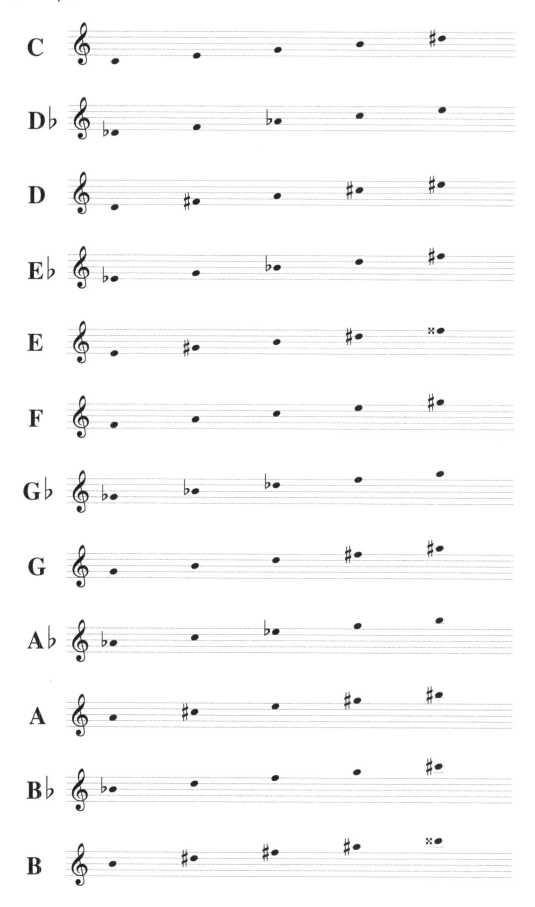

maj7♯9♯11

1 3 5 7 ♯9 ♯11

maj7♯9♯5

1 3 ♯5 7 ♯9

maj7♯9♯11♯5

1 3 ♯5 7 ♯9 ♯11

maj13♯11

1 3 5 7 9 ♯11 13

maj13#11#5

1 3 #5 7 9 #11 13

m7

1 ♭3 5 ♭7

m(maj7)

1 ♭3 5 7

m7♭5

1 ♭3 ♭5 ♭7

m(maj7)♭5

1 ♭3 ♭5 7

m9

1 ♭3 5 ♭7 9

m(maj9)

1 ♭3 5 7 9

m9♭5

1 ♭3 ♭5 ♭7 9

m(maj9)♭5

1 ♭3 ♭5 7 9

m9#11

1 ♭3 5 ♭7 9 #11

m(maj9)♯11

1 ♭3 5 7 9 ♯11

m11

1 ♭3 5 ♭7 9 11

m(maj11)

1 ♭3 5 7 9 11

m11♭5

1 ♭3 ♭5 ♭7 9 11

m(maj11)♭5

1 ♭3 ♭5 7 9 11

m13

1 ♭3 5 ♭7 9 11 13

m(maj13)

1 ♭3 5 7 9 11 13

m(maj13)♭5

1 ♭3 ♭5 7 9 11 13

m13♯11

1 ♭3 5 ♭7 9 ♯11 13

m(maj13)♯11

1 ♭3 5 7 9 ♯11 13

m7♭13

1 ♭3 5 ♭7 9 11 ♭13

m(maj7)♭13

1 ♭3 5 7 9 11 ♭13

m7♭5♭13

1 ♭3 ♭5 ♭7 9 11 ♭13

7

1 3 5 ♭7

7♭5

1 3 ♭5 ♭7

7♯5

1 3 ♯5 ♭7

7sus4

1 4 5 ♭7

9

1 3 5 ♭7 9

9♭5

1 3 ♭5 ♭7 9

9♯5

1 3 ♯5 ♭7 9

9#11

1 3 5 ♭7 9 #11

9♯11♯5

1 3 ♯5 ♭7 9 ♯11

9sus4

1 4 5 ♭7 9

11

1 3 5 ♭7 9 11

13

1 3 5 ♭7 9 11 13

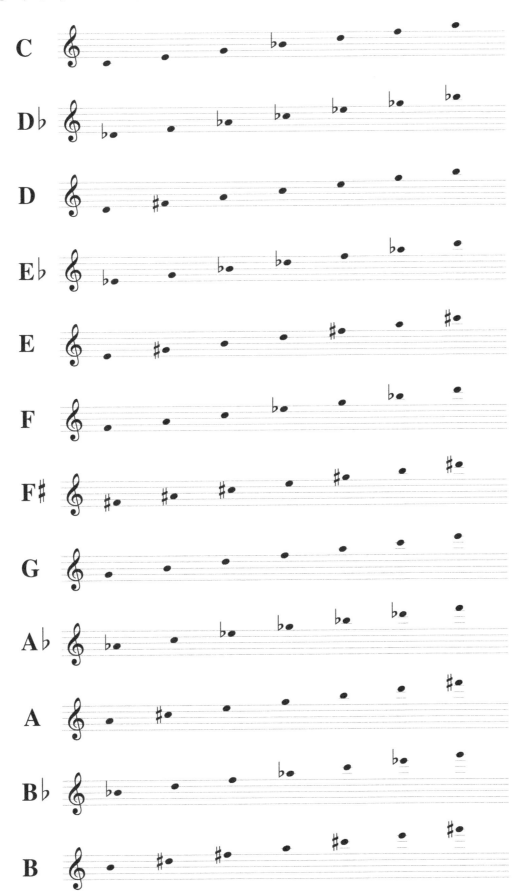

13♯11

1 3 5 ♭7 9 ♯11 13

13sus4

1 5 ♭7 9 11 13

7♭9

1 3 5 ♭7 ♭9

7♯9

1 3 5 ♭7 ♯9

7♭9♯9

1 3 5 ♭7 ♭9 ♯9

7♭9♭5

1 3 ♭5 7 ♭9

7#9b5

1 3 b5 7 #9

7♭9♯9♭5

1 3 ♭5 ♭7 ♭9 ♯9

7♭9♯5

1 3 ♯5 7 ♭9

7♯9♯5

1 3 ♯5 ♭7 ♯9

7♭9♯9♯5

1 3 ♯5 7 ♭9 ♯9

7sus4♭9

1 4 5 ♭7 ♭9

11♭9

1 3 5 ♭7 ♭9 11

7♭9♯11

1 3 5 ♭7 ♭9 ♯11

7♯9♯11

1 3 5 ♭7 ♯9 ♯11

7♭9♯9♯11

1 3 5 ♭7 ♭9 ♯9 ♯11

7♭9♯5♯11

1 3 ♯5 ♭7 ♭9 ♯11

7#9#5#11

1 3 #5 ♭7 #9 #11

7♭9♯9♯5♯11

1 3 ♯5 ♭7 ♭9 ♯9 ♯11

13♭9

1 3 5 ♭7 ♭9 11 13

13sus4♭9

1 5 ♭7 ♭9 11 13

13♭9♯11

1 3 5 ♭7 ♭9 ♯11 13

13#9#11

1 3 5 ♭7 #9 #11 13

13♭9♯9♯11

1 3 5 ♭7 ♭9 ♯9 ♯11 13

7♭13

1 3 5 ♭7 9 11 ♭13

7sus4♭9♭13

1 5 ♭7 ♭9 11 ♭13

7♭9♭13♭5

1 3 ♭5 ♭7 ♭9 ♭13

7♯9♭13♭5

1 3 ♭5 7 ♯9 ♭13

7♭9♯9♭13♭5

1 3 ♭5 ♭7 ♭9 ♯9 ♭13

P4+P4

1 4 b7

P4+A4

1 4 7

A4+P4

1 ♯4 7

P4+P4+P4

1 4 ♭7 ♭3

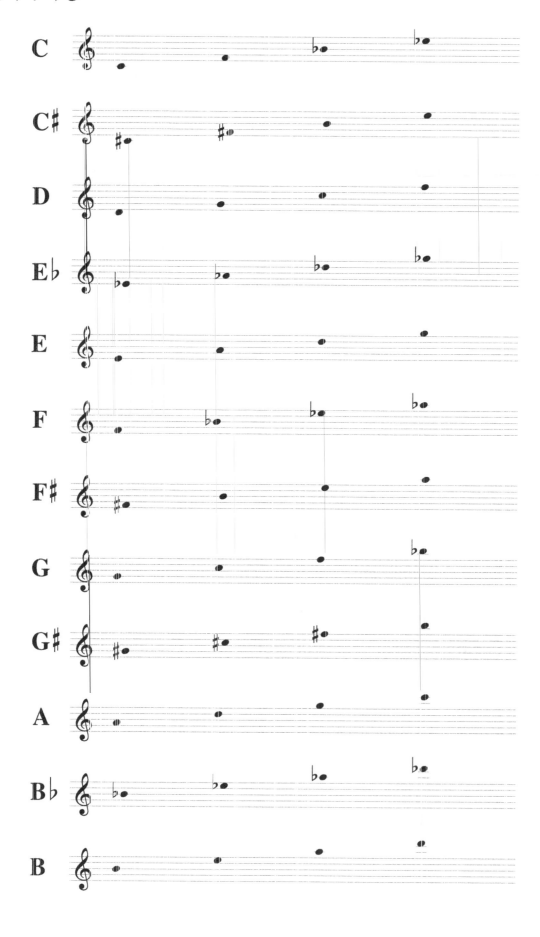

P4+P4+A4

1 4 ♭7 3

P4+A4+P4

1 4 7 3

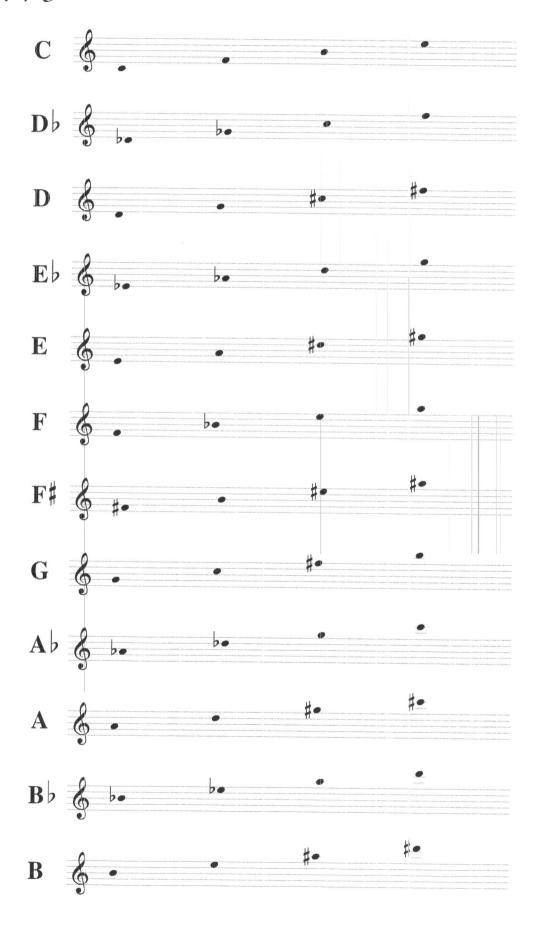

A4+P4+P4

1 ♯4 7 3

P5+P5

159

P5+P5+P5

1 5 9 13